P9-ASF-041

WITHDRAWN
No longer the property of the
Boston Public Library.
Sale of this material benefits the Library

The Watch Collector's Handbook

The Watch Collector's Handbook

by

M. Cutmore

David & Charles
Newton Abbot London
Vancouver

MAY 2 4 1978

NK 7484
· C 86

fine arts
5 | 78

ISBN 0 7153 7028 6
© M. Cutmore 1976

All rights reserved. No part of this
publication may be reproduced, stored
in a retrieval system, or transmitted,
in any form or by any means, electronic,
mechanical, photocopying, recording or
otherwise, without the prior permission
of David & Charles (Publishers) Limited

Set in 11 on 13 Baskerville
and printed in Great Britain
by Biddles Ltd, Guildford Surrey
for David & Charles (Publishers) Limited
Brunel House Newton Abbot Devon

Published in Canada
by Douglas David & Charles Limited
1875 Welch Street North Vancouver BC

CONTENTS

The photograph on the title-page shows a quarter-repeating verge watch by Wm Fredk Strigel, London. The movement is about 1750, but the watch was recased by a worker who wrote inside: 'Strigel, new case, January 18, 1843'. The case is of this period. The bell on which the hammers strike is in the back of the case. The movement is numbered 'BDFK'. The repeat action is operated by depressing the pendant. The movement has a dust cap (not shown).

PREFACE

This book introduces the reader to the world of watches and watch collecting. It also shows that the ordinary man with restricted means to support an interest has plenty of scope in what is sometimes regarded as an expensive hobby. Its intent is to enable the reader to appreciate the variety of options open to the collector and to provide him with the information he will need.

The historical survey sets the scene. The data in this chapter is based on the author's research and his experience of watches in museums and collections. Research-orientated readers would need to validate the early patents etc for themselves.

The photographs used as illustrations are not, however, of watches in museums but represent a sample of the watches that the author and his acquaintances have bought, sold and exchanged in the past few years. They are the sort of watches that are available without enormous expense; the sort that the ordinary collector can, with some effort, hope to find and purchase. Some of the photographs are of movements without cases. The movement of a watch is attractive in its own right and it is the timekeeper: the case is merely a box to protect the movement. This statement is not intended to devalue attractive casework but to highlight the fact that the purpose of a watch is to indicate time. Although casework has an important place in watch history the development of the watch over the centuries has been largely aimed at improving timekeeping, not at producing cases.

Chapter 4 suggests methods of repairing watches which

differ from those of the professional watch repairer: many of the watches and movements that a collector will acquire will have been discarded as useless or uneconomic to repair by professionals. If these methods give pleasure in their execution and satisfaction in their achievement then they may be regarded as successful. One most important point for the collector to ensure is that he does not through ignorance damage or destroy a watch that is valuable (financially or historically). It should be emphasised that work should not be commenced until the mechanism is identified and its mode of operation fully understood. Old watches and movements are becoming scarcer as more are broken up and those that remain should be treated with respect.

Chapter 1
HISTORICAL SURVEY

The history of watchmaking may be divided into periods. These periods are not equal in time but they represent eras in the development of the various skills involved in making a watch. The first lasts till 1600, the second from 1600 to 1675: a period of decoration. Then comes the new era of the balance spring, which may be divided into two periods: 1675-1700 and 1700-75. A period of intense mechanical development follows from 1775 to 1830 and finally the time from 1830 to the present is arbitrarily split at 1900 when the wrist watch starts to replace the pocket watch.

WATCHES BEFORE 1600

Mechanical clocks in which the driving power is obtained from a suspended weight date from the first half of the fourteenth century. Even a small clock with such a power source is not suitable as a portable timekeeper but it was not until the late fifteenth century that the coiled spring was used as an alternative means of power. If a watch is defined as a spring-driven timekeeper that is small enough to be carried on the person it is only necessary to reduce the size of the portable spring-driven clock for the watch to be born. Few early watches have survived and it is not possible to state exactly when or where the first was made. The earliest dateable examples are a German watch of 1548, probably by Caspar Werner of Nuremberg, and a French watch of 1551 by Jaques de la Garde. The German watch is in a drum-shaped or tambour case of gilded metal and the French watch is in an approximately spherical case. English and Swiss makes do not appear until a quarter of a century later when it is likely that refugee workers from France provided a stimulus for the local craftsmen. There is some documentary evidence for watches from Italy and the Low Countries contemporary with, or even predating, the German example but none have survived or, rather, none have yet been discovered and dated. The earliest watches had movements made of iron or steel in cast or fabricated gilt base-metal cases but brass soon replaced the iron for wheels and plates. The casework remained simple and by 1600 watchmaking was an established industry in most of Europe.

The timekeeping qualities of early watches are poor. The escapement, which is the mechanical device by which the

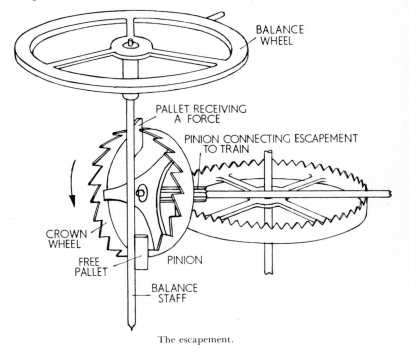

The escapement.

spring is allowed to unwind and so move the hand in small increments, is controlled by a balance bar or wheel. The balance rotates first in one direction and then in the other under the influence of the force delivered by the teeth on the crown wheel to the pallets on the balance staff. The pallets intercept teeth at opposite ends of a diameter of the crown wheel so that although the balance swings to and fro, the rotation of the crown wheel is continuously in one direction. This rotation is passed through the train (gearing) to allow the hand to rotate at the correct rate and in the correct direction against the indicating dial. The force delivered by the spring to the train and hence by the crown wheel to the balance-staff pallets depends on the quality and strength of the spring. It is not to be expected that early springs would give the same force when fully wound, partly wound or almost unwound. Consequently, the arc of swing of the balance, and therefore the rate at which the train rotates, will vary. If a long spring is used it is possible to obtain some control of the force delivered by only using the middle portion of the spring. The spring is partly pre-wound or set up by means of a rachet and pawl and is stopped from becoming fully wound by positive means and it is hoped that the force delivered by this middle portion is reasonably constant. The amount of set up may be varied with the rachet so that a measure of regulation can be obtained by selecting the portion of spring used. This method of control is inadequate and other devices are required to improve time-keeping.

An early attempt at further control of the force delivered by the spring was called the stackfreed. In the stackfreed additional friction is introduced to the mechanism by the pressure of an auxiliary leaf spring on a cam. The cam is shaped so that as the driving spring unwinds and the cam rotates the friction between the auxiliary spring and the cam is reduced to compensate for the reduction in force from the driving spring. The stackfreed is in evidence in early German

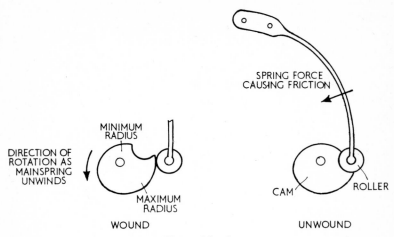

The stackfreed.

watches but French and English makers used a much better device known as a fusee. In this skilful design the spring is contained in a barrel. One end of the spring is attached to the barrel and the other (inner) end to a fixed arbor about which the barrel rotates. A length of gut (replaced later by chain) is attached, and wound on to, the barrel. The other end of the gut is attached to the fusee. The spring is wound by rotating the fusee, thereby coiling the gut on to the fusee which has a

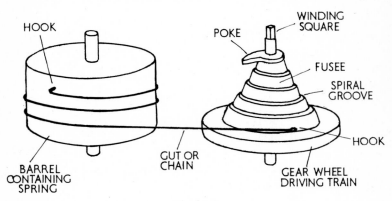

The fusee.

spiral groove cut on to its cone-shaped profile. When the
spring is fully wound the force which is transmitted to the fusee
by the gut acts at a small radius. As the spring unwinds the gut
is recoiled on to the barrel and the reducing spring force acts
at the increasing fusee radius. In a correct design the torque
(force multiplied by radius) applied to the fusee, and hence to
the train, is constant.

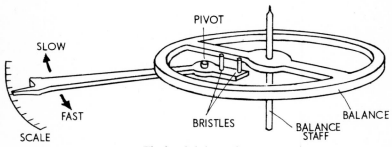

The hog bristle regulator.

Having made the force delivered by the crown wheel to the
balance as constant as possible with set up, stops, stackfreed or
fusee, regulation may be achieved by limiting the arc of swing
of the balance. The shorter the arc of swing, the quicker the
teeth of the crown wheel can escape past the pallets and the
faster the watch will go. The arc of swing was limited by stops
which needed some flexibility and were made of hog bristle.
The bristles were arranged on a pivoted arm so that their
position could be varied. When the balance arm banks against
the bristle the swing is stopped and, under the action of the
other pallet on the crown wheel, reverses its direction of
rotation.

Even if all these ingenious improvements had functioned
perfectly the friction in the train and in the escapement
between the pallets and the crown-wheel teeth would still vary
sufficiently to upset the timekeeping ability of the early watch.
This poor timekeeping was apparent in that only a single hand
was used to indicate the hour. The metal dial was engraved

with numerals at the hours and marks between these to show
the half hour. No glass was fitted and the dial often had raised
touch pins at the hours to enable the time to be felt in the
dark. Striking and alarm work were often included in these
early watches. The necessary mechanical arrangements merely
needed scaling down from the spring-driven clock.
Astronomical data and date mechanisms were also
incorporated by the end of the sixteenth century. Thus by 1600
the mechanical viability of the watch and the techniques to
obtain the best performance were well established in Europe
and there followed a period in which the development of
timekeeping was not greatly improved but in which both the
movement and the casework were given decorative attention.
Timekeeping improved slightly as the skill of the makers
increased. Thus, fusees and springs were better approaches to
the ideal and wheels less hampered by friction. Similarly, the
replacement of the ratchet and pawl for set up by a worm and
wheel gave finer control and a small dial indicator was fitted to
show the amount of set up used.

1600 — 1675

Early watches were worn on a chain about the neck. They were
neck watches and the pendant on the top of the case was
usually arranged so that the plane of the hanging ring was at
right angles to the dial of the watch. Since it was not possible to
take pride in superior timekeeping the decoration of the case,
which was a visible manifestation of the owner's wealth,
became important. Decorated watch cases were of gilt metal or
precious metal and were engraved, jewelled, pierced
(especially for striking or alarm) and enamelled. The cases of
surviving examples suggest that base metal was common but
this may be because the thick cases required to give rein to the
casemakers' skills were, if made of gold or silver, liable to be
melted down in hard times in subsequent centuries when the
watch itself was broken or considered inferior as a timekeeper.

The shape of the case changed from the simple tambour cylinder with a lid to a circular or sometimes oval body with hinged domed covers at back and front. There were several exceptions to this generalisation; one exception being the form watch, so called because the case was in the form of either a cross, a skull, an animal or a bird, another exception was the rock-crystal transparent case and a third the 'puritan' watch in a plain, oval, silver case made in England in about 1640.

Enamel work came in several forms. Champlevé enamel cases were first carved out and then the hollows were filled with coloured enamel. Another technique was to paint scenes in enamel on one or more surfaces of the watch covers, and a final variation was high-relief enamel in which the smooth enamel base had raised decorations of leaves or flowers superimposed. Translucent enamel was sometimes used to enhance an engraved case; the underlying design produced a different texture as light was reflected. Sometimes jewels were set in, or around, enamel scenes to highlight the effect or cases may just have been a receptacle for a spectacular display of jewels. From this brief description it is obvious that a watch case would pass through the hands of several craftsmen before the work was complete and the movement was finally fitted.

This delicate enamelling and jewelling led to the provision of a protective outer case often made of leather. To a certain extent the cover defeated the object of the decoration but it did not have to be worn since the pendant was attached to the inner watch case. If the cover was also worn, it was usually decorated with piqué work in gold or silver pins. A watch with two separate cases, both of which are designed to be worn, is called a pair-case watch. As the pair-case watch developed, the tendency was for the inner case to remain plain and all the decorative effort to be concentrated on the outer cover. The two-case trend coincides to some extent with the change from neck watch to pocket watch following the introduction of the waistcoat in gentlemen's dress. The hidden pocket watch needed less ostentatious decoration but it did require the pendant to be rearranged so that the hanging ring was in the same plane as the dial.

Glasses were fitted to cases from about 1620. At first they were held by tabs around the circumference of the hole in the dial cover, and a bezel split at the hinge was introduced a little later. Early glasses were of rock crystal; perhaps the advantage of seeing the time without opening the watch became apparent after this material had been used for some cases. Dials on enamelled case watches were themselves enamelled, usually with decoration or a scene. The hand was made of gold. On metal-cased watches the dial was usually engraved in the same metal or champlevé with an engraved or matted centre. The hand was of blued steel.

Since the watch owner had to open his watch for winding and regulation there was also a need to make the movement as attractive as the case and dial. All the brasswork — plates, wheels, pillars and cock — could be gilded. This contrasts well with the blued steel of the set-up worm, springs and screws. The main decorative features were the balance cock and pillars. The balance cock forms the upper bearing for the balance staff and was originally a simple curly C or S design pinned to a block on the plate. As the balance bar disappeared in favour of the balance wheel, the cock became larger to protectively cover the whole wheel. It was circular or oval shaped and was screwed to the plate being supported by an enlarged foot. Both the cock and the foot were pierced with open scrollwork. The space not used on the plate by cock and foot, set up, etc, was used to engrave the maker's name and place of business. The pillars separating the plates have considerable variation in shape becoming progressively more elaborate. Spiral, round, columnar, baluster, tapering Egyptian and tulip shape are most common. Additionally, between the plates, the spring winding stop above the fusee was given a decorated pivot.

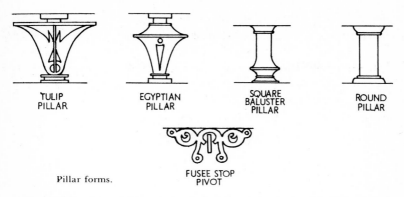

TULIP PILLAR   EGYPTIAN PILLAR   SQUARE BALUSTER PILLAR   ROUND PILLAR

Pillar forms.   FUSEE STOP PIVOT

By 1670 the pocket watch with pair cases had become established and consisted of a decorated outer cover with a plain inner case in gilt metal, silver or gold or perhaps decorated with enamel or pierced for striking and alarm. A glass was fitted over the dial. The movement was gilt with worm set up and a gilt pierced cock, decorated pillars and fusee stop pivot, and a replacement for the fusee gut was making an appearance in the form of fine chain with a hook at either end for attachment. The watch was ready for the next important step forward.

1675 — 1700

The invention of the mainspring as a power source gave birth to the watch in about 1500. The next significant step in its history was the application of the spiral spring to balance control by Huygens in 1675. This single improvement changed the watch from a poor timekeeper with a daily variation measured in scores of minutes to a moderate timekeeper where daily accuracy could be assessed in minutes. There was considerable controversy about this invention both in 1675 and in later times when historians have investigated rival claims. The principal argument is whether Hooke or Huygens should be credited with the invention. Both men were involved in experiments with spring control of the balance from about

1660 but Huygens appears to have been the first to apply the spiral form. Some of Hooke's early work was concerned with straight springs but it is difficult to adequately reconstruct a time scale for information exchange in those days of poor communication.

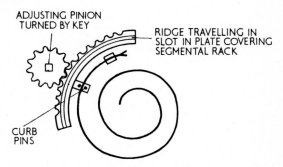

ADJUSTING PINION
TURNED BY KEY

RIDGE TRAVELLING IN
SLOT IN PLATE COVERING
SEGMENTAL RACK

CURB
PINS

The principle of Tompion regulation.

There is no doubt that in 1675 Hooke was collaborating with the craftsman Thomas Tompion to produce a watch with a spiral balance spring. There is also no doubt that Tompion continued to apply the spiral spring from this date onwards. Tompion gained a reputation as a watchmaker partly as a result of his use of the balance spring coupled with the use of Hooke's wheel-cutting engine which enabled him to make wheels more accurately and partly for his superb workmanship. Tompion used a regulator, which enabled the active length of the balance spring to be varied by curb pins operated by a segmental rack. This allowed the time that the balance took to make a vibration to be adjusted to give accurate timekeeping. Shortening the spring made the watch go faster, while lengthening it made the watch go slower. Tompion was also a good works manager who succeeded in subdividing the work involved in making a watch into skilled and less skilled tasks so that he could reserve his own efforts for the more important aspects of manufacture.

The action of the balance spring was to use the impulse

given to the balance wheel (by the crown wheel through the pallets) to coil up the spring, so bringing the balance to rest. The spring then uncoiled, returning the balance to the centre position. The impulse on the other pallet caused it to uncoil further until the balance again came to rest. Recoiling returned the balance to the initial position. The time taken to complete a full vibration depends on the mass and mass distribution of the balance and on the mechanical properties of the spring. In the early days of the application it was hoped that the balance vibration was isochronous. This means a time of vibration which is independent of the arc of vibration. It was found that this was not true and further it was discovered that the temperature of the watch affected its timekeeping ability due mainly to the variation of the elasticity of the balance spring with temperature. This fault could only become apparent with the improved timekeeping of the watch. It was also found during this era that the position — pendant up, pendant down, etc — of the watch affected its timekeeping. The balance spring opened a new vista of problems.

Notwithstanding these disadvantages, the improvement in timekeeping achieved by the balance spring was so great that watches were given two hands and dials subdivided into minutes. The dials were still marked with Roman numerals at the hour but an additional minute ring was provided with slightly smaller Arabic numerals indicating each five minutes around the outer perimeter. Before this method of indication was finalised other experimental dials and methods were tried (and still are in modern times) but the now conventional arrangement was found to be most suitable. Regulation by Tompion's method meant that the set up lost its place on the top of the plate and was put between the plates where it was rarely required except when fitting a new mainspring. The small dial indicator was retained in Tompion's design and used in the same way to determine how the regulator was set. Subsequent to the addition of the balance spring to the watch, a fourth wheel was added to the train. The extra wheel meant that the watch would run for a day between windings rather than the half day achieved by the original three-wheel train.

1700 — 1775

The period from 1700, when the balance spring watch was well established, until 1775 was one in which the English watchmakers were acknowledged to be the best. Disturbing political influences on the Continent aided the skill of the English craftsman to establish this supremacy. Before the turn of the century the mechanism for the repeating watch was perfected independently by Barlow and by Quare and just after the turn of the century, de Facio, a Swiss, together with two emigré Frenchmen (both named Debaufre) took out an English patent for cutting and piercing jewels for bearings. The repeating watch was made in considerable numbers both in England and on the Continent but jewelling was confined to England and was rare. Even by 1750 its use was largely restricted to the upper bearing of the balance staff in the cock. Friction in other bearings was reduced by lubrication and bearing holes in plates were cupped from the middle of the century to provide a small reservoir which restricted the migration of the oil. Dust caps were fitted to movements early in the century for with the improvement in timekeeping it became noticeable that the intrusion of foreign matter in the movement caused the rate of the watch to deteriorate. The cap had holes in it to allow regulation and winding without the need for complete removal and movement exposure.

Dials in this period (1700-75) at first continued champlevé but were slowly replaced by a white, enamelled type with black numerals so that by 1750 champlevé was rare. The enamel dials continued the practice of Roman hour numerals with Arabic minute indication but the minute numerals were tending to become smaller as a prelude to their eventual disappearance. Some dials, either of European origin or destined for export, had arched or arcaded chapter rings. Hands were of blued steel or gold in various forms of beetle and poker. The hour hand is known as a beetle hand because of the insect-shaped decoration at its outer end whereas the minute hand is straight and undecorated and is known as a poker hand. Cases were relatively simple on the early watches with superior timekeeping but as this timekeeping ability became the accepted standard and repeating work was not uncommon case decoration again became fashionable. In this period repoussé outer cases were often in evidence. Repoussé work is achieved by hammering a scene into the metal from inside the case so that a high-relief decoration results. The result has a similar look to fine casting. Some enamel work continued but was often restricted to a small scene rather than over the whole case. Some outer cases were covered in tortoise-shell, either plain or inlaid with precious metal, others were covered with translucent horn painted on the underside with fine patterns of ferns or flowers or with scenes. The pendant became more elegant and the hanging ring became a bow, stirrup shaped and pivoted to the pendant rather than looped through. Glasses were snapped in from early in the century.

Movement decoration continued in spite of the fact that many were covered with a dust cap and the inner cases were sometimes pierced to allow winding without opening. The cock at first became very large in diameter (balance wheels were larger) with a broad sector-shaped foot and much of the rest of the plate was covered with pierced decorative pieces. On the Continent, the cock had no foot but was instead a circular bridge screwed to the plate at either end of a diameter. The early years of the eighteenth century were the peak of movement decoration and as time passed the foot became smaller and the diameter decreased; both, however, remained pierced. From about 1750 the foot ceased to be pierced and extra decorative pieces became uncommon. Movement decoration never increased again. The small dial indicating

The development of verge-watch style c1750-1850. All the watches have fusee and chain. The *upper left* watch is by T. Moore, London, no 9291 and is in a silver-gilt inner case hallmarked 1758 with an outer case of underpainted horn. The movement pillars are square baluster. The hands, except for the date indicator, are not original. The *upper right* watch is by Stoakes, London, no 15148 and is in an inner silver case hallmarked 1781 with an outer case of repoussé silver. The movement has square pillars and a bridge cock. The dial is arcaded and the watch is in the 'Dutch forgery' style. The *lower left* watch is by W. Hall, London, no 122 and is in silver pair cases hallmarked 1771. The movement has square pillars. The dial is typical of the period, the Arabic numerals outside the Roman numerals becoming less emphasised. The hands are beetle and poker style. *Lower right* — maker unknown. The watch is in a double-bottomed silver case hallmarked 1844. Smaller than the others shown, it is typical of the later forms of the verge watch. The movement pillars are cylindrical; the hands may not be original.

The maker of the watch *shown above* is not known. This watch, in silver pair cases hallmarked 1827, is much larger than the others shown which is typical of the verge watch of the 1800-30 period. The Arabic numerals on the dial are not as common as Roman numerals. The movement has cylindrical pillars.

the state of the regulation continued throughout the period and the maker's name and origin were still engraved in the vacant spaces. Pillars became progressively simpler from the elaborate tulip form and by mid-century small square baluster pillars were common and some plain cylindrical pillars were in evidence. The decoration of the fusee stop pivot continued and the end of the spring operating the catch holding the movement in the inner case was often quite elaborate.

By 1700 no change in the basic verge escapement of the watch (crown wheel and pallets) had taken place since its inception. No doubt experimental escapements had been tried but none were considered viable. For example, there is a patent of 1695 to Booth (sometimes called Barlow), Houghton and Tompion for a new escapement but no watches have survived. Booth and Houghton were associated with Tompion, as was Graham, and this early patent may have helped

Graham to introduce the horizontal or cylinder escapement in 1726. From the timekeeping aspect this escapement was undoubtably an improvement on the verge but it was more difficult to make and was fragile. Friction is still present in the design and the cylinder watch did not displace the verge in England nor even approach it in numbers made. Some eminent makers used it in addition to Graham who quite naturally concentrated his efforts on the new design. The cylinder was taken up on the Continent, particularly in France and Switzerland. At the end of this period (1700-75) Lepine used it to produce a much thinner watch in which the top plate was replaced by a number of bars or bridges. Lepine also dispensed with the fusee and used a going barrel in which the spring container drove the train directly. The use of stopwork and the improvement in spring quality combined with the cylinder movement enabled adequate timekeeping without the fusee. The smaller, thinner watches were considered more desirable on the Continent but English makers continued to seek quality by using the fusee in both the verge and the cylinder movement. This could be considered a first step in the decline of the English as the premier watchmakers, but the symptoms were not to be apparent for many years to come.

1775 — 1830

Geographical position at sea is determined by latitude and longitude. Latitude is quite easily evaluated by observations of sun or stars but longitude is more difficult because it is necessary to know the Greenwich time at which the observation is made. The earth takes 24 hours to rotate through 360 degrees so that a change in longitude of 1 degree is represented by 4 minutes difference in time. For example, the local time of noon is obtained from observations giving the instant of the maximum altitude of the sun. If the Greenwich time of this altitude is one hour after local noon then the longitude is 15 degrees west of Greenwich. The problem during a voyage is to be sure that the watch or clock indicating Greenwich time is correct or is capable of being corrected. This is not difficult in these modern days of radio communication but in the eighteenth century the timekeeper could only be set by an observation at a shore station of known longitude. A timekeeper that has a constant rate of loss or gain can be corrected but one which has a variable rate due to friction, environmental changes, etc, cannot be corrected and is useless. The invention of the mainspring made the clock portable and suitable for use at sea; the invention of the balance spring improved timekeeping by an enormous amount but the clock or watch was still not capable of an accuracy suitable for navigation.

In 1714 an enormous reward was offered by the Board of Longitude (established by Act of Parliament) to the inventor of a suitable portable timekeeper. The instrument would have to determine longitude to within thirty minutes of arc of a great circle at the end of a voyage from Great Britain to the West Indies to qualify for the maximum award of £20,000. This meant that the timekeeper would, after this long voyage, have to be within two minutes of the correct time with due allowance for the rate of loss or gain previously stated. The story of the effort to qualify for this award has no place in this review but with this colossal sum of money available it is not surprising that many attempts were made to construct a timekeeper that would satisfy the requirements.

The successful maker was John Harrison who spent virtually the whole of his life constructing a series of timekeepers designed to fulfil the requirements of the Board of Longitude. He succeeded with a voyage from Portsmouth to Jamaica taking from 18 November 1761 till 19 January 1762 with a corrected error of one and a quarter minutes of longitude. It took him until 1773, with a second demonstration in 1764, to get the full reward. Although Harrison's marine timekeeper was successful his contribution to navigation was effectively

limited to demonstrating that it was possible to design and
construct an accurate device. His mechanisms were too
complex. Other eminent horologists, notably Le Roy and
Berthoud on the Continent and Arnold and Earnshaw in
England, contributed to the production of the practical
marine chronometer and, in watch form, the pocket
chronometer. Their designs included a spring or pivoted
detent escapement in which the balance is completely
detached from the rest of the train (except at the instant it is
receiving impulse), a helical balance spring which can be
made isochronous more easily than a spiral spring, and maintaining power in the fusee so that the timekeeper continued to
go whilst being wound (Harrison's designs also had

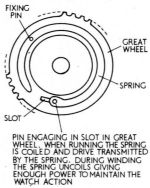

Maintaining power.

maintaining power). All designs incorporated some form of
temperature compensation. The form which survived was the
cut, bimetallic balance and by 1800 the pocket chronometer
was a readily available accurate watch.

Some of the improvements were incorporated into the
ordinary pocket watch. Maintaining power was used with the
fusee from about 1800 and, if the other timekeeping qualities
merited it, a bimetallic balance was fitted. This design of
balance attempts to compensate for the change in elasticity of

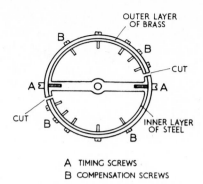

A TIMING SCREWS
B COMPENSATION SCREWS

The bimetallic balance wheel.

the balance spring with temperature by making the balance rim of two different metals fused together. The outer layer of the rim is made of brass which has a higher coefficient of expansion with temperature than the inner layer which is made of steel. The rim is cut in two places near to the balance arms so that the free ends will move inward when heated and outward when cooled. This alters the mass distribution of the balance which will slightly change the time of vibration. Compensation screws are arranged around the rim to give a measure of control to the correction. The timing screws at the ends of the balance arms are not for compensation but are used to adjust the initial mass distribution so that the fundamental time of vibration is correct. With carefully set timing screws and correct compensation a regulator is not required and the watch is free sprung. This delicate adjustment is restricted to pocket chronometers and other high-grade watches.

In 1775 the verge watch was still the mainstay of the industry. In the succeeding fifty years a number of escapements were invented or developed from earlier ideas. This period of intense mechanical development was possibly inspired by the success of the chronometer makers who had demonstrated that accurate timekeeping was possible.

The limitations of the verge watch were a result of the friction in the escapement. The vibration of the balance was always affected by the contact between the crown-wheel teeth and the pallets. Similarly, in the cylinder escapement there was friction between the escape-wheel teeth and the cylinder during the vibration of the balance. To improve the time-keeping qualities of a watch an escapement was needed in which the balance was detached from the train during the vibration. This was achieved in the detent escapement. Before the development of the detached escapement there were a number of other non-detached designs which were tried and which could be considered an improvement on the verge from the timekeeping standpoint but which were not successful replacements because they were not detached and because they were harder to make and maintain. The verge is a simple, tough escapement. Three of these escapements with friction were made in sufficient numbers to merit discussion.

The duplex escapement invented in about 1720 by Dutertre, and modified to its common form around 1750, was used mainly in England from the closing years of the eighteenth century to the middle of the nineteenth century for high-grade watches. The duplex escape wheel has two separate sets of teeth, one for locking the train and one for giving impulse to the balance. It only allows escape once per vibration (as does the detent) and the audible tick is easily recognisable.

An escapement invented by Debaufre in about 1700 has two escape or crown wheels which give impulse to a single inclined plane pallet on the balance staff. It did not achieve great popularity but variations known as the chaffcutter, Ormskirk, club-foot verge and dead-beat verge were developed and made in England in the early nineteenth century. Some of these use two wheels and some two pallets.

Finally, among non-detached escapements there is the rack lever invented in about 1720 by Abbé de Hautefeuille and improved by Litherland in England in 1791. In the rack lever the balance staff is fitted with a pinion which is permanently and positively engaged with a rack at the end of a pivoted lever. Impulse is given to an anchor-shaped piece fitted to the lever. The escape wheel has pointed teeth and the design could

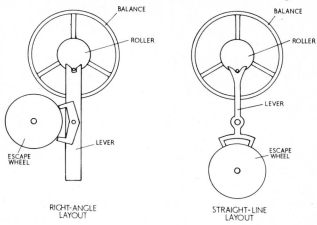

Lever escapement layout.

be considered as a direct application of the anchor escapement to a watch. This type of escapement can be seen in longcase clocks but the most common form in the clock has recoil whereas that in the rack lever watch is dead beat. Rack lever watches were made from about 1790 to 1840.

It may be observed that each of these escapements was conceived around 1720, about forty years after the balance spring had transformed timekeeping, but none of them was sufficient an improvement on the verge to merit further attention until the period of mechanical interest of 1775-1830. In the intervening time the makers of chronometers had produced a viable, accurate watch and sometime in the period 1750-60 Mudge had designed the detached lever escapement. Strictly speaking the Mudge design was not perfectly detached because there was a possibility of friction between the lever and the balance-staff roller. Mudge initially applied his escapement to one or two clocks and is only reputed to have applied it to a single watch in about 1770. He was more interested in the problem of marine timekeeping and devoted his skill to solving this problem rather than developing the escapement which was destined to be the solution to cheap and accurate timekeeping.

Several other eminent makers made a few examples of lever watches in the period up to the turn of the century but none made it in significant numbers. It seemed that the possibility of friction was a stumbling block. Most of these makers changed Mudge's original right-angled layout to a straight-line arrangement. Peculiarly, the Mudge arrangement was revived and used almost exclusively in the English lever watch whereas the European makers used the straight-line layout. The missing essential to the lever watch in these early essays was draw. It is not clear who invented draw in which the escape wheel teeth are shaped to pull and hold the lever into engagement with the escape wheel thus locking the train. The holding of the lever ensured that there was no possibility of slipping into contact with the balance-staff roller so that the escapement was truly detached and the requirements for good timekeeping (no friction during the vibration) were satisfied.

In 1814 Massey invented a form of lever escapement in which he used the right-angled layout of the rack lever and Mudge. In his escapement the rack lever pinion (on the balance staff) is replaced by a single tooth and the rack by a single slot. After the tooth receives impulse from the slot the balance becomes detached. Some Massey levers do not have draw so that friction is still possible, others have draw. In later forms the single tooth becomes a jewel supported initially at both top and bottom to form a crank and finally supported only at the top. The escapement in these final forms is also known as the crank lever.

Sometime around 1825 the detached table roller lever watch evolved when the crank of the Massey lever was replaced by a thin cylindrical roller with an impulse jewel projecting from

An English table-roller lever watch by Wymark, London, no 3898, in a double-bottomed, silver case hallmarked 1827. It has a fusee with maintaining power and an oversprung balance. The movement pillars are cylindrical and the movement has a dust ring. The dial is silver with raised gold numerals.

the base of the cylinder. In this form, with draw, the ultimate replacement for the verge escapement in England had arrived. The layout of the English lever watch retained the right-angled arrangement of Mudge, the rack lever and the Massey lever. This distinguished it from the European straight-line layout for the next hundred years—its life span. Another variation of the lever appeared in 1815. It was detached and looks similar to the table roller. However the train is unlocked by two pins on the roller (one for each direction of vibration) and impulse is given to a slot in the roller by a pin on the lever. Exactly the reverse of the table roller in which the slot in the lever gives impulse to the jewel pin on the roller. The construction was more difficult than the table roller design and the Savage two-pin escapement did not survive.

The development of new escapements led to some modification in the layout of the watch. The improvement in timekeeping merited the use of the seconds hand and this became conventionally placed indicating on a small subsidiary dial above the six hour mark. The seconds hand required the train gearing to be arranged so that one wheel rotated at the correct rate and was sited correctly. Jewelling was widely used in the train and some extremely attractive large jewels were fitted on the visible plate. This is sometimes called Liverpool jewelling and indicates the importance achieved by the Lancashire watch industry at this time. Ratchet and pawl set up under the dial was used rather than worm and wheel. The plates were arranged in a more convenient form for assembly and repair. On the dial plate a small bridge bar was used so that the bottom bearings of the fusee and the fourth wheel (seconds-hand wheel) and the complete third wheel could be fitted after the assembly of escapement and centre wheel. On the other plate the barrel was given a separate bridging plate so that it could be fitted or the mainspring renewed without the watch being completely stripped. Maintaining power was generally used and on some watches a chronometer type bimetallic balance was fitted, but this was rare.

Decoration in all watches of this period was becoming minimal. The watch was now a timekeeper. Cocks were solid with some attractive chiselling and engraving and with some variety in shape. This may be used to help to identify the type of escapement likely to be found between the plates. The cocks were often engraved 'patent' or 'detached'. These varieties were short-lived. Since dust caps were normally fitted, little other decoration was used as only the cock was visible. Pillars were cylindrical and watches tended to be thinner than the 1770 verge but larger in diameter to accommodate the seconds hand. The regulator was amended to dispense with the segmental rack of Tompion's design and the small indicating dial. Instead there was a simple lever with curb pins embracing the balance spring which was rotated by hand. The centre of rotation of the lever coincided with the balance axis so that movement of the lever moved the curb pins around the arc of the balance spring. The end of the lever passed over a scale engraved on the plate to show the amount of regulation. The scale was often marked 'fast' and 'slow' at its ends to make regulation simpler and more accurate.

Many of these improvements and changes were used in the verge watch. In particular, the bridges, for ease of assembly, were added and this required the third wheel of the train to be moved to the other side of the contrate wheel. The regulation was made similar to the new simple design and the worm set up was replaced by ratchet and pawl under the dial. Set up was usually only required on the rare occasions when the mainspring was renewed and at this time the dial could be removed to give access. The cock became simpler with a solid foot and eventually with no piercing. Plain cylindrical pillars were usual and, to keep in style but not in timekeeping ability, a seconds hand was sometimes fitted. The watch diameter increased substantially but the thickness was not reduced.

Pair cases were not always used in watches with the new escapements and by 1830 this type of case was rare except on the old-fashioned verge. Where pair cases did exist they were usually of silver or gold with various shaped pendants and stirrup-shaped bows. Decoration was unusual on either inner or outer case. The alternative single cases used with the new escapement watches were of various designs but decoration was minimal and usually confined to engine turning on the back and a milled circumference of the centre band. The common form of single case had a double bottom. The watch was wound by opening a hinged back which revealed a second fixed bottom pierced by a winding hole. The movement was hinged to the top of the case front as in the inner pair case but the bezel holding the glass had a separate hinge adjacent to the nine hour mark. Glasses were thinner and flatter to match the larger diameter flat dial and the small flat in the centre of the glass disappeared. The pendant was a spherical knob often pierced by a push piece which released a spring catch holding the back closed. The bow was circular.

Dials were usually white enamel with a single set of numbers indicating the hours. Both Arabic and Roman numerals were used but Roman continued to be the more common. The dials tended to be less domed because the diameter was greater. Dials with seconds hands were flat. Hands became simpler. The beetle and poker gave way to an hour hand with spade-shaped end and the minute hand was a simple pointer. Seconds hands had a counterpoise with a circular end. The materials used were still gold or blued steel.

The English watch of 1830 was severe but attractive and a good timekeeper. Although a large variety of escapements was available the English table roller lever was beginning to become established. On the Continent, developments were different. It has been explained how the cylinder escapement and the Lepine barred-movement design led to a thinner watch there. In general this trend continued with wider use of the going barrel rather than the fusee. The fusee was not completely discarded and was retained in many of the traditional verge watches of this period. Verge watches are generally smaller than their English counterparts often because of the case design. The pair case was abandoned in the quest for minimum size and often a single bottom case was used with no dust cap and winding through the dial. Cocks were small pierced bridges and the silvered regulator dial continued. The European verge watch presented a very plain and uncluttered movement.

Although the rack lever and duplex were originally European in concept they did not receive the late-eighteenth century attention that was given them in England. A variation known as the Chinese duplex was made on the Continent at the end of the period under discussion. In this design the train was

A Continental verge watch of about 1800 in a silver case. The bridge cock, coqueret and regulator figure plate are typical. The movement pillars are five-sided baluster. The crown wheel has adjustable bearings at both ends. The watch is wound through the dial and there is usually no access through the case back. The movement is fitted with a fusee.

only allowed to move on every other complete balance vibration and the sweep seconds hand moved forward in uncomfortable looking steps of one second. Two further escapements received more attention on the Continent than in England. These were the virgule and the Pouzait. The virgule has an escape wheel with teeth standing up from the plane of the wheel giving impulse to a comma-shaped piece on the balance staff. The Pouzait is a form of lever escapement which had some following in Switzerland and France. The cylinder watch continued to be made in greater numbers on the Continent than in England but, as in England, there was a move towards the lever.

In 1787 Breguet produced lever watches in France. There is the possibility that the concept of the lever in France by Julien Le Roy preceded Mudge's first essay but at the moment there is too little evidence to be certain. There is no doubt about Breguet's work which is well documented. His design used a straight-line layout with a cut, compensated balance. It is to be expected that anything produced by Breguet would have some innovation and be executed with workmanship of the highest quality. He is probably the most famous European maker noted for his workmanship and style. His best-known work includes ruby cylinder watches, the design of an overcoil for the end of a spiral balance spring giving isochronous vibrations, the shock-absorbing 'parachute' balance staff suspension, a self-winding watch and the tourbillon watch in which the complete escapement assembly rotates about once every few minutes to minimise positional (pendant up or pendant down, etc) errors in the watch. Breguet's life spanned the period of intense mechanical development and he was no mean contributor.

European lever watches show another important difference from the English design apart from the straight-line layout. The English design used an escape wheel with pointed teeth. The pallets on the working surfaces of the anchor fitted to the lever were steeply angled. This meant that lift giving impulse to the balance was provided solely by the lever. In the European design the lift was divided between the lever pallets and the escape-wheel teeth so that these teeth were not pointed but had a broad or club foot.

European cases and dials were in keeping with the slimmer watches being produced. Even in the traditional verge the pair case was not used and certainly in the new designs the fusee was omitted in the interest of a slim watch in a small elegant case. Engine turning was used as in England but there was more emphasis on case decoration than in England where the watch was severe but attractive. European dials were usually white enamel, often with Arabic numerals in greater evidence and with a wider variety of hand forms than would be found on English watches.

In Switzerland the cylinder was supreme and the makers were steadily moving towards volume production. However, the decisive steps along this path were not taken until the next period and in 1830 the position on the Continent is summarised by stating that in France the lever was becoming established in straight-line form and in Switzerland the cylinder was poised for its successful hundred-year run.

1830 — 1900

During the first quarter of this period the (English) lever watch became established in England. It was still possible to obtain watches with other escapements but they became increasingly rare and by 1850 the lever was supreme. Even the verge was faltering after a three-hundred-year history. Changes in the lever watch meant that there was considerable variation in internal and external appearance. By 1860 the form of the lever itself had changed from the early straight-sided design to a curved one. Many watches were obviously made in the same workshop and then finished by the 'maker' whose name was engraved on the plate. In the traditional full-plate layout, the balance and balance cock are above the plate giving a thick watch. Watches were thinned by using a three-quarter or half-plate movement. In the three-quarter plate, the balance, lever and escape wheel were placed with separate cocks in a space obtained by cutting away a section of the plate. In the half plate the fourth wheel also has a separate cock. The fusee was continued until the last decades of the century. The concessions to thinning had been made.

Changes in the methods of winding occurred continuously and many of the ideas came from the previous era of mechanical activity. In 1814 Massey had produced a push or pump winder with a rack operated by pushing the pendant turning a ratchet on the fusee or going barrel. In 1820, Prest, who worked for Arnold (the son of the chronometer maker, Arnold), patented a system with a bevel drive through the pendant connected to a going barrel and in 1827 Berrolas patented a pull-wind system with a recoil spring operating rather like a mower starter. None of these systems was completely satisfactory because a key was still required to adjust the hands. This problem was overcome in some cases by adding a hand-setting train operated by a wheel protruding from the side, or back, of the movement. Other variations exist but the successful winding systems came from the Continent.

The first man to devise winding and hand setting through the pendant was a Swiss maker, Audemars, in 1838. Variations and improvements followed from other Swiss makers (Philippe, Lecoultre and Huguenin) who produced the shifting-sleeve and rocking-bar arrangements. Initially the change of mode from wind to hand set was by means of a small push piece at the side of the winding button but this extra piece was not required in the design in which pulling the winding button effected the change of mode. The drawing shows four arrangements. There are other varieties involving different layouts and which mode was engaged by button pushing or pulling and it was many years before the pull-button shifting-sleeve form became the norm. Self-winding watches were conceived by Perrelet (a Swiss) in 1770 and Breguet produced them from 1780 but the 'pedometer' wind did not become a serious pocket-watch device and was discarded until required for wrist watches. Perhaps there was insufficient motion in the average eighteenth-century pocket.

The keyless-winding and hand-setting system allowed some change in case design. It was not necessary for the front to hinge open for hand setting and so a snap-on bezel was introduced. Similarly, it was only necessary to open the back for regulation or servicing and as this was normally the job of a watchmaker the double bottom to the case was abandoned. Instead the hinged back was snapped firmly shut with a small lifting piece to allow it to be opened. The dust cap on the movement was no longer required and was replaced by a

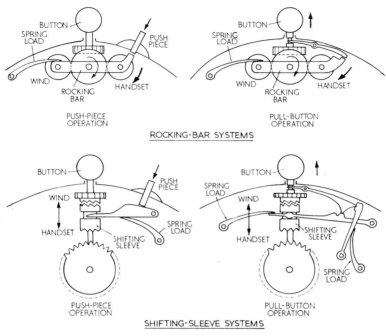

BUTTON
SPRING LOAD
PUSH PIECE
WIND
ROCKING BAR
HANDSET

PUSH-PIECE OPERATION

BUTTON
SPRING LOAD
WIND
ROCKING BAR
HANDSET

PULL-BUTTON OPERATION

ROCKING-BAR SYSTEMS

BUTTON
PUSH PIECE
WIND
HANDSET
SHIFTING SLEEVE

PUSH-PIECE OPERATION

BUTTON
SPRING LOAD
WIND
SPRING LOAD
HANDSET
SHIFTING SLEEVE

SHIFTING SLEEVE

BUTTON
SPRING LOAD
WIND
SHIFTING SLEEVE
HANDSET
SPRING LOAD

PULL-BUTTON OPERATION

SHIFTING-SLEEVE SYSTEMS

Keyless winding

small, hinged cover fitted inside the case back. The movement was no longer hinged to the case but was held in place by screws. When the bezel and screws were removed the movement could be passed out through the front of the case.

In England, keyless winding was rare in this period mainly because most of the systems discussed were only suited for use with the going-barrel watch. In the 1890s there was some tendency to change from the fusee to the going barrel but the English makers still continued to favour the traditional key-wind watch. The internal style of the watches keeping to the full-plate layout changed little except that the cocks reached a minimum of decoration and there were one or two variations in the regulation layout. Liverpool jewelling gave way to less obvious small jewels. The external style changed as the

An English table-roller lever watch by J. D. Williams, Merthyr, no 27353, in a double-bottomed silver case hallmarked 1873. A typical mid-Victorian lever watch of moderate quality with a cut compensated balance and fusee with maintaining power.

Victorian period progressed. The case and dial became heavier to the eye, losing the austere elegance of 1830. Dials in 1830 were usually flat and a number of recognisable styles evolved, resulting in the familiar Roman numerals with recessed seconds hand. Hands became slimmer. The quality of the English lever watch of the middle- and late-Victorian period, taking both timekeeping and workmanship into consideration, was good and such a watch is still capable of giving satisfactory daily performance a century later.

The use of the seconds hand caused stop mechanisms to be added to some watches. In the early designs a simple internal stop piece operated on the balance rim or the lever. Later in the period there were a group of watches often marked, quite incorrectly, 'chronograph'. In this group the dials were divided in quarters or fifths of seconds and the rate of vibration was increased to enable these divisions to be realistic but when the sliding stop piece on the case was moved the same internal

The *left-hand* watch has a cylinder escapement and plated brass case. Although the dial is labelled 'chronograph' it is not, as the stop piece locks the train and stops the watch; there is no reset and start action. Continental. The *right-hand* watch is a chronograph with separate stop, reset and start action for the centre seconds hand. The mean-time hands continue even when the stop is operated. The watch has a Swiss lever escapement and is in a silver case of about 1920. Both watches have a going barrel.

arrangement stopped not only the sweep seconds hand but the whole watch. Timing techniques with these watches were crude. There were more expensive watches with separate trains for the seconds hand and the normal mean-time hands and these were much better. However, a true chronograph should be capable of being stopped, reset and restarted whilst the mean-time hands continue. (Similarly a stop watch should have the stop, reset and restart facility but without mean-time indication.) This capability was designed in 1844 by Nicole but it was a further eighteen years before the familiar three-push system on the winding button was devised. The all-important resetting was achieved by a heart-shaped cam moved by the pressure of a spring. The single train chronograph drove the seconds hands by friction wheel engaged and disengaged by the push button.

Towards the end of the period all the varieties — repeaters, moonwork, alarm, striking, musical, automata, jaquemarts, multi-dial, day, date, month, stop — were available and many watches had more than one of these complexities. A large proportion of these watches were Swiss with lever or cylinder escapement and many had decorated cases. One English refinement was the karrusel patented in 1892 by Bonniksen. This was a simpler version of the Breguet tourbillon which compensated for positional error.

So far, the most significant happenings of the period, which were to outdate the traditional English watchmaking techniques and to see the establishment of the Swiss and American machine-made watch industry, have been bypassed. It is difficult to understand how the Swiss and Americans could see the market potential of cheap machine-made watches when England, where the industrial revolution was born, could not. In particular, the annual export figures achieved in the twentieth century by Switzerland (24 million in 1950, 41 million in 1960 and 63 million in 1967) show the magnitude of the missed opportunity.

From about 1840 onwards, machine-made watches with interchangeable parts were produced in Switzerland. The designer of the machine was Leschot, the man who had introduced draw into Swiss lever escapements and designed standard tools to make lever escapements. Leschot's machine was based on a pantograph so that the holes in the plates were always in identical places and thus parts became inter-changeable. The secret of his machine was kept by the firm who commissioned the work and besides selling watches they had a successful market for movements.

The idea of the machine-made watch travelled to America and there was developed to a volume-production system which then returned to Switzerland. The way in which these ideas travelled across the world was new. In 1851, the Great Exhibition was held in London and this was followed by exhibitions in Paris in 1855, London in 1862, Paris in 1867 and Philadelphia in 1876. Further exhibitions followed, but it was the Philadelphia exhibition which enabled the Swiss to realise the magnitude of the American challenge and to take appropriate remedial action. Thus in Europe, the Swiss applied volume-production methods to both the cheap cylinder and the more expensive lever watches in small fob form for ladies and pocket form for gentlemen. They were sold in ever-increasing numbers throughout the world gaining new customers from their attendance and medal winning at the various exhibitions.

The American watch industry is a post-1850 phenomenon. Before this date few watches were made in America, most were imported from Europe either as parts for assembly or as complete watches. Harland made approximately two hundred watches in about 1800 and tariff restrictions in the period 1809-15 encouraged Goddard to make watches but as soon as the restrictions were removed European imports again dominated the market. Goddard is reputed to have made about five hundred watches. Starting in 1837, the Pitkin brothers produced about a thousand machine-made watches but they did not compete with the Swiss-made watches because their parts were not interchangeable. There were a few other makers, such as Custer, but their products were numbered in tens of watches so that they are insignificant in terms of quantity.

The breakthrough came from Dennison, Howard and Curtis who, perhaps realising the superiority of the Swiss methods, sent Dennison to Europe to learn all he could. In 1850 they founded the American Horologe Company in Roxbury which successively became the Warren Manufacturing Company, The American Watch Company in 1859, the American Waltham Watch Company in 1885 and, in 1906, the Waltham

American watches. *Upper left and right,* a watch with a Swiss lever escapement by the Peoria Watch Co, Illinois. It has a compensated balance, a going barrel and fine adjustment of the regulator by worm and wheel. The case is made of silver with a screw-on front. The hands are adjusted by a rocking bar operated by a lever hidden under the bezel. The *lower left* watch by the American Waltham Watch Co has a Swiss lever escapement, a compensated balance, a going barrel and fine adjustment of the regulator. The gold-plated case has a screw-off back. The *lower right* watch is by the Waterbury Watch Co and is a late example of their duplex watch. It does not have the long mainspring and rotating movement. The pressed-out escape wheel is shown separately. The dial is made of paper and the watch case of plated steel. The hands are set by pushing and rotating the winding button.

Watch Company which continued in business until 1950 — a one-hundred-year span. From the beginning their products were lever watches wound by key, button wind being introduced in 1870. Eventually they had no less than thirty factories. The Waltham company was basically a producer of quality watches and they were joined in this field by Howard in 1857, Elgin in 1864 (Elgin were called The National Watch Company till 1874) and the Hamilton Company in 1892. A peculiarity of all American watch companies is the variety of names used on dials and movements. The personalised names came from partners of firms and the changes of company names from amalgamations, financial problems, changes of site, etc. There was also a tendency to use monograms instead of names on dials. The better-quality American watches of this period were lever watches and they often had quite elaborate methods of regulation control with fine screw adjusters of various designs, and attractive engine engraving on the movements. Cases were double bottomed in the European style for key wind but there was also an interesting style with a screw-on front with button wind using rocking bar hand adjustment. In order to allow the movement to be hinged from the case to give access to the regulator, the winding stem was partially withdrawn by pulling the button.

An alternative line of development was followed by The Waterbury Watch Company. Founded in 1878 by Benedict and Burnham, the company was called Waterbury from 1880 to 1898, the New England Watch Company from 1898 to 1912 and in 1914 it was sold to Ingersoll who finally failed in 1922. At the beginning in 1878, Buck obtained a patent for what was to become The Waterbury Watch. It was a cheap, machine-made design with only 58 parts and a very long mainspring which was infamous for the time it took to wind. This spring was coiled behind the movement which rotated like a tourbillon carrying the minute hand around with it. The dial was printed on paper, covered in celluloid and the duplex

Left, a pin-lever watch by F. E. Roscopf with a silver-plated cast-metal case of about 1910. The casting on the back of the case is of a railway engine and the bezel is surrounded by the words 'Veritable montre chemin de fer'. The watch has a going barrel. So has *right,* a Roscopf movement, late 19th century. The escape wheel and lever can be clearly seen.

escapement had a pressed out wheel. This remarkable watch was discontinued in 1891 although the duplex escapement continued to be used with conventional winding until the end of the century. The demise of the company was caused by too cheap an image. The cheap-watch idea was also pursued by Ingersoll who started trading in 1892 selling a clock watch complete with folding winder inside the case.

Thus it can be seen that in America during the period 1850-1900 the quest for volume production at a price and quality to compete with Swiss products led to the formation of a large number of watch companies. Many of these companies failed to survive and were sold, combined or taken over. There was no signing of movements by individual makers as in Europe since from the very start the concept was one of the machine-made factory product. This devotion to production had its effects in Europe for after the challenge of this approach was realised by the Swiss they amended their own methods and eventually eliminated most European competition.

The cheap watch had developed independently in Switzerland in the form which was eventually to become worldwide. Roscopf designed and produced a pin-pallet lever watch in 1867. He presented one of his watches at the Paris Exhibition and the award of a medal contributed to his success. Roscopf used the minimum number of parts, a three-wheel train, simple keyless winding with hand adjustment by finger and cheap metal (as opposed to gold or silver) cases. His watch was patented abroad but was available to Swiss makers who were able to produce similar designs. Thus Switzerland began to present large numbers of pin-pallet, cylinder and lever watches which together satisfied all price levels of the world market. The pattern of watchmaking for the first half of the twentieth century was set.

1900 ONWARDS

From 1900 onwards there are few new technical developments. Probably the most significant was work in the metallurgical field. A change in temperature causes changes in the dimensions and in the elastic properties of materials, which called for the application of temperature compensation in the form of the cut, bimetallic balance. Although this design of balance gives an enormous improvement, it still leaves a middle-temperature error between, and errors beyond, the two temperatures at which the balance can be designed to give correct compensation. These errors may be given an allowance based on the rate of gain or loss. The allowance will vary with ambient temperatures.

The early approaches to eliminating this error were by means of auxiliary compensation devices in which the inward or outward motion of the balance arms due to change in temperature was modified by extra fittings. Many of these compensations were discontinuous in action and only partially corrected the error and even the best continuous-action designs were not perfect at all temperatures. In 1900 metallurgical investigations into the properties of nickel-iron alloys enabled Guillaume to produce an alloy which was used in the compensated balance in place of steel. This alloy has a temperature coefficient of expansion of such a value that when it is combined with brass in a cut, compensated balance (known as a Guillaume balance) the middle-temperature error is virtually eliminated. Guillaume had previously produced an alloy called Invar which had a negligible temperature coefficient of expansion and he continued his work to tackle the errors caused by variation in elastic properties in a better way. In 1912 he deduced that it was possible to make an alloy for balance springs which would have no change in elasticity with temperature. Experimental work to produce the alloy Elinvar proceeded and from 1919 it was possible to use a monometallic balance of Invar controlled by an Elinvar spring. These alloys were not ideal because their other properties such as hardness and suitability to being formed were not as good as those of the metals that they were replacing but, following Guillaume's lead, modern metallurgy has produced more suitable materials, some of which also have the desirable properties of being non-rusting and non-magnetic.

Changes in the non-technical field were dominated by the change from the pocket watch to the wrist watch. A wrist watch had appeared in 1571 and in 1809 but it was not until the early years of the twentieth century that any quantity was produced. The tendency to change was enhanced by the 1914-18 war in which a watch on the wrist proved much more convenient than one in the pocket and in which the new design had a chance to prove its reliability. From the manufacturer's view, the first problem was one of scale. However the volume-produced, Swiss, cylinder fob watch used movements of such a size to show that the problem was not insoluble and early wrist watches made in Switzerland used the cylinder movement. The Swiss lever wrist watch followed some years later. By 1930 the ratio of wrist watches to pocket watches produced was of the order 50 to 1. Winding was by button and hand adjustment by rocking bar or shifting sleeve. The dial was arranged so that the winding button was at three o'clock. However watches can be found with the button at twelve. These may be fob conversions by a local watchmaker to satisfy a customer or produce an up-to-date line to sell. The strap lugs in early designs (and conversions) were simple wire loops added to what was virtually a minature pocket watch case or fob case without decoration. Hinged or snap bezels and backs were used, the snap design giving better access to the movement which was removed from the front of the case. Dials were white enamel or metal without decoration but the numbers were sometimes treated with a luminous compound. Watch glasses began to be made from a transparent plastic material which was less fragile than glass but which scratched more easily and tended to become yellowed with age.

Although the pocket watch continued until the end of the 1939-45 war production after 1945 was minimal. The demise of the waistcoat as a common form of dress was a contributory factor to its decline. The change from the pocket watch coupled with the economic effects of large-scale continental production and the depression effectively finished the production of watches in England by 1930 and it was not until after the end of the 1939-45 war that a new machine-based industry was established. In the early years of the century English watchmakers had started to use the going barrel but some continued to use keywind. There were also a number of firms selling watches with their name on the dial or plate but also somewhere in small letters were the words telling the story, 'Swiss made'. This practice continued throughout the period under discussion.

The cylinder movement was another casualty of the period. Having demonstrated the viability of the wrist watch the development of the miniature lever movement meant that there were three types of movement looking for room in a market which really only needed two. For the expensive fully- or partly-jewelled watch the lever was ideal and for the cheap watch the pin pallet was satisfactory. Thus, after two hundred years the cylinder movement had completed its useful life.

In 1945, the European watch industry was dominated by Swiss-produced wrist watches with lever movements. After this date the quality wrist watch began to acquire the complexities that had been available in pocket watches. In particular, automatic winding was widely applied using Perrelet's principle. This was not the first modern application of automatic winding for Harwood had used Perrelet's ideas in 1924 and made wrist watches in the Isle of Man. Harwood had completely dispensed with the stem winder with shifting-sleeve hand adjustment but the later Swiss designs kept the winder/hand adjuster in the majority of cases. One of the problems in the development of automatic wrist watches is the excess of movement available at the wrist. The chronograph also became available in wrist form often coupled with datework, alarm work, moonwork, etc. Watches became shock resistant, waterproof, acceleration proof, able to function on land or sea, in the air, under the water, in space under weightless conditions and on the moon.

Despite the Swiss domination there are watch industries in most of the major countries in Europe but with standardisation and the operation of multi-national companies it is not easy to distinguish national characteristics in the products of any one country. The pattern of development in America was similar to that in Europe. The need for pocket watches slowly disappeared as the wrist watch became established. American companies continued to proliferate and to succeed or fail as in the years before the turn of the century. The depression

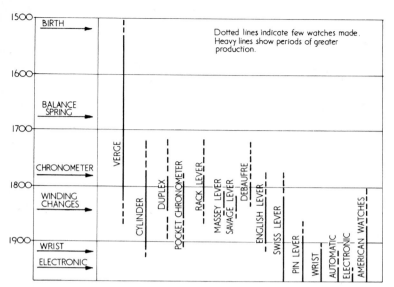

Chronological chart.

stabilised the situation so that the post-war industry is based on fewer large companies. The history of these companies is complex and it is not easy to trace all the changes. The pattern of production became similar to that in Europe with the lever escapement for the more expensive watch backed by the pin pallet for the cheaper range. New developments in America were largely concerned with electrical applications. The battery-powered watch was available in the period from about 1952 (also in Europe) but this was only an alternative form of automatic watch. The new design was the electronic watch — a result of the developments of very small electronic components. In this design the balance-spring and balance-wheel method of incrementing power was replaced by electronically induced resonant vibrations of a tuning fork, a completely new concept of timekeeper. This principle has been developed in Europe using crystal vibrators with a much higher frequency of vibration than the tuning fork to give considerably increased accuracy. The rate of vibration of the crystal system may be as high as 2,359,296 per second which is an interesting figure when compared with the average balance-spring-controlled wrist watch at 2.5 per second.

The concluding diagram to this historical survey shows the life span of the watch escapements discussed and some of the significant happenings in the four and a half centuries reviewed.

Chapter 2
TECHNICAL SURVEY

A watch is designed to indicate time by the rotation of hands against a calibrated dial. The power causing the hands to rotate is obtained from the mainspring coiled in the barrel. The power is transmitted through a (gear) train which allows the hands to rotate at a different speed to the barrel, the hour hand going more slowly and the minute hand faster. In a gear train the ratio of the rates of rotation of two meshing wheels is the inverse of the ratio of the numbers of teeth. The drawing shows the arrangement of a watch with a normal four-wheel train.

The first wheel in the train is known as the great wheel and is either the fusee wheel or, in a watch with a going barrel, the barrel wheel. The great wheel meshes with the centre-wheel pinion which is on the arbor or shaft of the centre or second wheel. On the end of the same wheel shaft is the cannon pinion to which the minute hand is attached. The cannon pinion is a good, but not rigid, fit on the centre-wheel shaft so that the hand may be set without moving the train. The centre wheel must be constrained to rotate once per hour. The hour hand is driven concentrically with the minute hand through a separate twelve-to-one step-down gear train known as the motion work. The motion work is situated between the dial and the dial plate whereas the train wheels are situated between the plates. Continuing with the train layout, the centre wheel meshes with the third-wheel pinion, which is on the same shaft as the third wheel, which in turn meshes with the fourth-wheel pinion, which is on the same shaft as the fourth wheel. This fourth

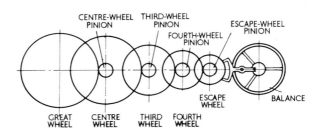

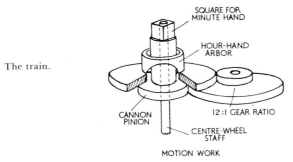

The train.

MOTION WORK

wheel has the seconds hand fitted to its shaft and must therefore be constrained to rotate once per minute. These four
wheels have their numbers of gear teeth chosen so that the
seconds hand and minute hand rotate at the correct relative
speeds but if the mainspring is wound the train would rotate at
enormous speed. The speed is regulated to the correct value by
the rate of vibration of the balance wheel through the
escapement.

The action of an escapement allows the escape wheel to
rotate one tooth at a time. The escape-wheel shaft carries a
pinion which meshes with the fourth wheel of the train, so that
the train is allowed to rotate in small increments which give the
correct average speed. The different designs of escapement
may be broadly divided into two groups: frictional rest
escapements and detached escapements. Examples from either
group may have recoil or dead-beat characteristics, and there
are also examples from either group known as single-beat

escapements, these allow only one escape-wheel tooth to pass or escape per balance vibration compared with the more usual two per vibration. In the frictional rest escapement, the vibration of the balance is never free from friction forces owing to contact with the escapement; examples are the verge and cylinder escapements. In the detached escapement the vibration is free of the train except at the instants of unlocking the train and receiving impulse to maintain the vibration. The detached escapement has considerable advantages in time-keeping qualities; examples are the detent and lever escapements. Recoil characteristics are exhibited by designs in which the escapement, and hence the train, moves backwards for an instant during the escapement action; examples are the verge escapement and the lever escapement with draw. An escapement which is dead beat does not have this recoil action, the cylinder escapement being an example.

A number of different escapements are now considered in detail. Not all these designs were made in the same numbers and the duplex, detent, Debaufre, rack lever, Massey lever and Savage lever are less common than the rest. (Some uncommon escapements are not described.)

Verge Escapement

The drawing shows the verge escapement, used from the sixteenth century to the nineteenth century. It is a frictional rest, recoil escapement. Before its use in the watch it was used in clocks and its origins are not clear. The escape wheel is sometimes called the crown wheel because of the shape of the teeth. It is arranged to engage with two pallets on the balance staff or verge. The shaft of the crown wheel is at right angles to the remainder of the train so that the fourth wheel with which the crown-wheel pinion meshes is a contrate wheel, with teeth in the vertical plane of the staff rather than a conventional gear wheel. The crown wheel has an odd number of teeth (usually thirteen), and as it rotates the pallet at the upper end of the verge is pushed by one of these teeth, causing the

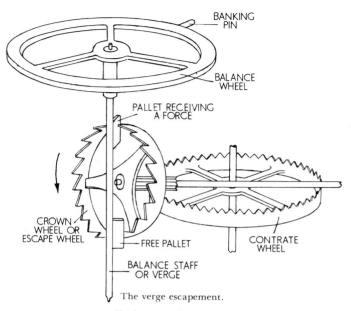

The verge escapement.

balance to rotate until the tooth escapes past the end of the pallet. The train and balance are momentarily free but the rotation of the verge has been just enough to cause the lower pallet to engage with a crown-wheel tooth at the opposite end of the diameter (the pallets are slightly more than a right angle apart), and the freedom ceases. The rotation of the balance is stopped by this lower pallet but not instantaneously and there is a small arc of motion in which the crown wheel and train rotate backwards or recoil. The influence of the mainspring causes the crown wheel to resume its normal direction of rotation and to push the lower pallet out of its path until the tooth escapes and the sequence is restarted. The crown-wheel teeth are undercut to ease the recoil action. If the pallet does not succeed in bringing the balance to rest, banking will occur, when a small pin in the balance rim strikes a projection on the balance cock (upper bearing) thus avoiding excessive swing.

Although the balance and verge are vibrating and

continually reversing their direction of motion the fact that the escaping teeth are at opposite ends of a crown-wheel diameter means that the rotation of the crown wheel and the train is undirectional.

Cylinder Escapement

The cylinder escapement was introduced in 1726 by Graham. This may have been as a result of his earlier association with Tompion, Booth (or Barlow) and Houghton who had a patent in 1695 for a new escapement which could be considered a forerunner of the Graham design. The cylinder escapement was also called the horizontal escapement to distinguish it from the vertical or verge escapement.

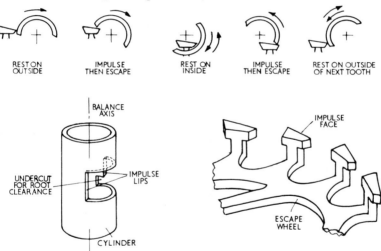

The cylinder escapement.

The escape wheel has a vertical shaft and usually has fifteen teeth which project vertically from the rim of the wheel. These teeth engage with, and pass through, a special slot cut in a hollow cylinder fitted into the balance-wheel shaft. The working portion of the hollow cylinder has approximately half its circumference removed so that a tooth may escape by passing through the cut-away portion of the cylinder at the appropriate moment during the balance vibration but may rest on the outside or the inside of the cylinder during the remainder of the vibration. The retained half of the cylinder is undercut to allow the tooth root clearance when the tooth rests on the inner surface of the cylinder.

The escapement is a frictional-rest, dead-beat design in which impulse is given to the balance twice per vibration by the sloping surface of the escape-wheel tooth acting on the edge of the hollow cylinder. The drawing shows the sequence of events in the action of the escapement.

Duplex Escapement

The duplex escapement derives its name from the original double escape wheel used in the design. The more common form described here has two sets of teeth on a single escape-

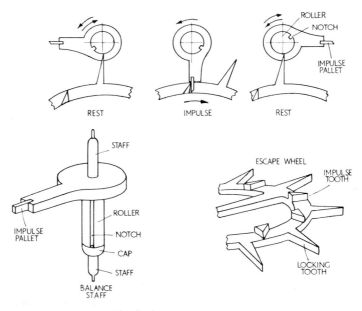

The duplex escapement.

wheel rim. One set of teeth is for locking the train and the other for impulsing the balance. The teeth are set alternately around the rim. Impulse is given once per balance vibration since the locking teeth only escape when the balance is rotating in the opposite direction to that of the escape wheel. The impulse is given by the inner ring of raised teeth on the rim of the wheel striking the impulse pallet which projects from the balance shaft or staff. The outer, pointed teeth projecting from the escape-wheel rim are allowed to escape by passing through a vertical slot cut in a jewelled roller fitted around the balance staff. Escape is in two steps; a very small movement as the tooth slips across the width of the slot and a much larger movement as the tooth escapes from the slot. This motion is stopped as the next pointed tooth comes to rest on the roller surface. On the return swing of the balance the slot slips past the tooth resting on the roller without permitting it to escape. This tooth is pressing on the roller for almost the complete vibration and the escapement is frictional rest with single-beat action. The drawing illustrates the action of the escapement.

Detent Escapement

The word 'detent' is defined in the *Concise Oxford Dictionary* as a 'catch by removal of which machinery is set working'. This definition is almost adequate to describe the escapement used in the pocket chronometer and shown in the drawing. The detent is sprung or pivoted about one end and it holds the escape wheel and train locked by means of a jewel (known as the locking pallet) standing up from its surface. The balance staff carries two pallets and as the balance swings the discharging pallet momentarily pushes the passing spring against the detent which moves to release the escape wheel. The rotation of the escape wheel allows impulse to be given to the impulse pallet on the balance staff by an escape-wheel tooth before the train is again locked by the locking pallet on the detent. On the return swing of the balance the passing spring merely flexes as the discharging pallet passes and does not unlock the escape wheel and train. Thus escape only occurs once per vibration. During the vibration the balance is detached except at the instant of unlocking and impulse and the escapement is a detached, dead-beat design with single-beat operation.

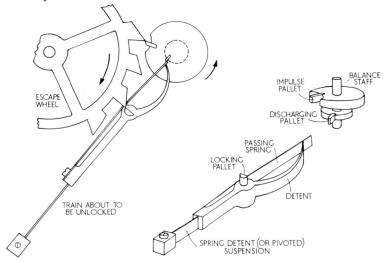

ESCAPE WHEEL

IMPULSE PALLET

BALANCE STAFF

DISCHARGING PALLET

PASSING SPRING

LOCKING PALLET

DETENT

TRAIN ABOUT TO BE UNLOCKED

SPRING DETENT (OR PIVOTED) SUSPENSION

The detent escapement.

Early pocket chronometers designed by Arnold used a pivoted detent but later he used a spring-detent design. Earnshaw also used a spring-detent design. Most other English pocket chronometers seen will also have spring-detent escapements but continental makers usually favour the pivoted detent. The relative merits of the designs are difficult to assess but one advantage that the spring detent offers over the pivoted detent is that the escapement needs no lubrication except for the balance and escape-wheel pivots.

Debaufre-type Escapements

These escapements, like the verge escapement, use a contrate wheel as the fourth wheel and at first sight might be taken as a verge design. Closer inspection will reveal that the simple

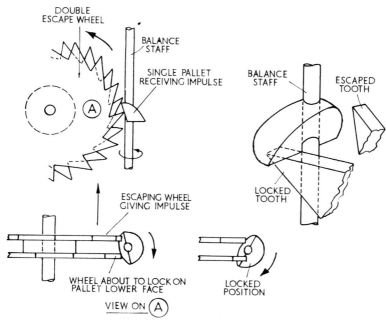

The Debaufre-type escapement.

crown wheel and verge has been replaced by other designs.
Various arrangements involving one or two pallets attached to
the balance staff with an escape-wheel system comprised of a
single or double crown wheel, or a single or double saw-tooth
wheel, have been used. The drawing illustrates one variety.
The basic idea was conceived by Debaufre in 1704 but the
main use occurred at the end of the eighteenth century and the
beginning of the nineteenth century in England. The
escapements are frictional rest and have a variety of names
such as dead-beat verge, club-foot verge, Ormskirk and
chaffcutter.

The pallets are horizontal, D-shaped and have inclined
edges. They alternately receive impulse from an escape-wheel
tooth on the inclined edge and lock the train on the horizontal
surface. If two escape wheels are used, the single pallet receives

the impulse as one wheel escapes and then locks the other wheel. If two pallets are used the single escape wheel gives impulse to the one pallet before being locked by the other pallet.

Lever Escapements

The basic principle of the lever escapement is shown in the drawing. The lever is pivoted at A. Impulse is given to the pallet B by the escaping tooth C. This impulse is transmitted to the balance. The rotary motion of the lever created by the impulse causes pallet D to intercept tooth E and lock the train. On the return swing of the balance the lever is pivoted back to allow tooth E to escape as it gives impulse to pallet D which is again transmitted to the balance. The lever motion causes pallet B to intercept tooth F to lock the train. This continuous rocking motion of the lever allows teeth to successively escape. There are a number of varieties of the design. Those discussed are mainly concerned with the connection of the lever to the balance staff but two have differences from the pallet and escape-wheel design shown above.

The original lever designs did not have draw which is

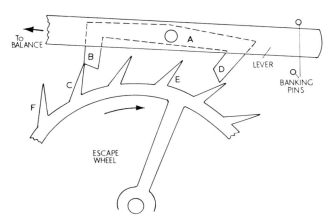

The principle of the lever escapement.

essential in all detached forms of the escapement to avoid accidental motion of the lever which would result in friction between the lever safety piece and the balance-staff roller. The friction would disturb the timekeeping quality of the escapement. Draw consists of shaping the escape-wheel teeth and lever pallets so that the lever is pulled towards the escape wheel. The lever cannot be drawn in too far because banking pins are placed to restrict the angular movement. When the lever is deliberately moved by the return swing of the balance, draw causes a slight recoil in the action. Draw is probably absent if the locking faces of the lever pallets have convex curvature but the use of straight-faced pallets cannot be used to construe the presence of draw. It is unlikely that any lever made after 1820 will lack draw.

In the form shown in the drawing above the escape wheel has pointed teeth and the actions of lifting and pivoting the lever are entirely a result of the slope on the pallets. This is characteristic of the English forms of the lever escapement discussed (the rack, Massey, Savage and table roller levers) whereas in the Swiss lever the shape of the escape-wheel teeth will be seen to be modified to share the lifting action between pallet and teeth and in the pin lever the escape-wheel teeth are steeply sloped to give most of the lift.

The lever escapement descriptions that follow are not exhaustive of the types that may be found. However, although there are other rare types, the majority of the variations seen will only be trivial. For example, the English layout may be used with the Swiss-type escape wheel which shares the lift between lever pallet and escape-wheel tooth. Similarly levers may have different shapes with counter balances etc, but the action and acting surfaces are the same. A variation which is of more interest but which would require careful measurements is in the proportions of lever lengths, roller diameters, etc, which will affect the forces involved in the action of the escapement and the time taken for each part of the action to occur.

Rack Lever Escapement

The rack lever design was conceived by Abbé de Hautefeuille in 1722 but the particular form discussed here was patented by Litherland in 1791. It was made in England in some numbers in the late eighteenth and early nineteenth centuries. The operation of the escapement is essentially that described above and shown on page 62 and the lever is connected to the balance by a rack which is permanently engaged with a pinion on the balance staff. Thus the escapement is not detached nor is it really a frictional 'rest' design.

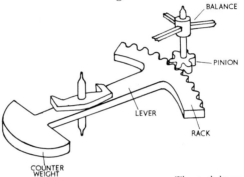

The rack lever escapement.

The large mass of the rack at one end of the lever is counter-balanced by a D-shaped piece at the other end. Many rack lever escape wheels are of large diameter with 30 teeth instead of the more usual 15 teeth. This large wheel is associated with a three-wheel train and is therefore not suited to the use of a seconds hand in the conventional way. The three-wheel train will also mean that the direction of rotation of the escape wheel is opposite to that of the more usual fifteen-tooth escape wheel. The figure above shows the lever and balance staff arrangement. It may be seen that the balance staff, lever shaft and escape-wheel shaft are planted so as to form a right angle. This arrangement is characteristic of developed forms of the lever escapement in England.

Massey Lever Escapements

In 1814, Massey invented a detached lever with the right-angled layout mentioned above. It has been suggested that the original concept was developed from the rack lever by forming a single-toothed 'pinion' on the balance staff to engage with a two-tooth 'rack' on the lever end. This original form is shown in the drawing, part a, and in it the roller on the balance staff is entirely made of steel which is in harmony with the idea of the single-tooth pinion. Some of these early original-form Massey lever watches also used the large-diameter, 30 tooth, escape wheel with a three-wheel train. Draw is not found in early Massey levers but was introduced and is usually present in the two later forms.

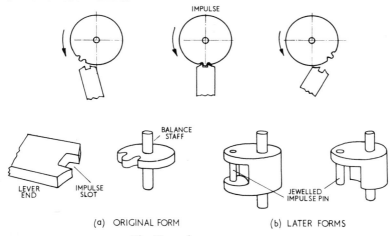

(a) ORIGINAL FORM   (b) LATER FORMS

The Massey lever escapement.

In these subsequent developments the single tooth of the pinion or roller became a jewel forming a crank to engage with the lever slot and the escapement is sometimes called a crank lever or crank roller escapement. In this form (drawing above, part b), the significance of the Massey escapement as a lead toward the final form of the English table roller lever escapement is clear. Although Mudge and others had made lever watches between 1770 and 1800 the numbers were minimal and the escapement did not seem to be making any headway as an alternative to the verge or cylinder. Massey's design, which survives in some quantity, especially in the later forms, really set the lever on the path to success. This may have been a result of a combination of circumstances rather than the design but the dominance of the lever could be considered to start in 1814.

The action is similar in all three forms. As the balance swings through the centre arc the roller tooth or jewel engages with the slot in the end of the lever and unlocks the escape wheel. The jewel then receives impulse from the slot (transmitted from the escape wheel) and the balance becomes detached for the remainder of the action. The escapement is locked by one of the pallets on the lever during the detached portion of the vibration. On the return swing the roller tooth or jewel again picks up the lever slot, unlocks the train and receives impulse. While the balance is in the detached portion of the vibration the lever should remain drawn in to the escape wheel. Should it move from this position because of the absence of draw or the failure of the draw action then the curved surfaces of the outer sides of the lever's slotted end (lever horns) will rest on the cylindrical surface of the balance roller preventing the train from unlocking and damaging the escapement. This safety action will introduce friction and destroy the advantage of the detached balance in timekeeping ability since for the faulty part of the action it is frictional rest in character. When the return swing of the balance brings the roller tooth or jewel back to the appropriate position the engagement with the lever slot will restore correct action so that the friction is only a temporary feature.

Savage Two-Pin Lever Escapement

The Savage two pin is another detached lever escapement invented in about 1815. It uses the right-angled layout but the arrangement for locking and unlocking the train and for

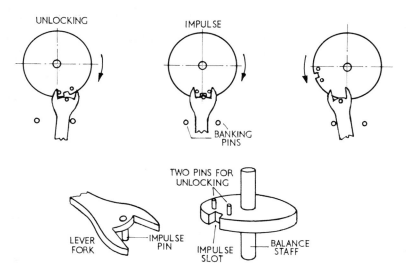

The Savage two-pin escapement.

impulse is different to other forms of lever. As shown in the drawing, the balance staff is fitted with a roller which has two pins protruding from its surface. Situated centrally between these pins is a slot. The lever end has a wide opening with a jewelled pin just below the centre point of the bottom edge of the opening. As the balance swings, one of the pins on the roller enters the jaws of the wide lever opening. This unlocks the train and impulse is transmitted from the escape wheel to the balance roller as the pin on the lever engages with the slot in the roller. The train is then locked by one of the lever pallets in the usual way. The balance becomes detached for the remainder of the vibration except for the repetition of the action on the return swing when the second pin on the roller effects the unlocking of the train. Should the lever become displaced during the detached portion of the vibration, the lever jewel will rest on the side of the balance roller giving a safety action with frictional rest until the normal unlocking and impulse restore the situation.

English Table-Roller Lever Escapement

The table-roller lever is the final form taken by the detached lever escapement in England. It first appeared in about 1823 and had a lifespan of approximately one hundred years. It is shown in the drawing below. The right-angled layout is again used and the escape-wheel teeth are pointed. The slot end of the lever is a different shape to the Massey and Savage forms. The roller on the balance staff has a single elliptical or D-shaped jewel protruding from its surface. As the balance vibrates through the central position the roller jewel comes into contact with the lever and engages the slot. The train is unlocked and impulse is transmitted from the escape wheel via the lever to the roller jewel. The balance then swings detached from the lever and train until the action is repeated on the return swing.

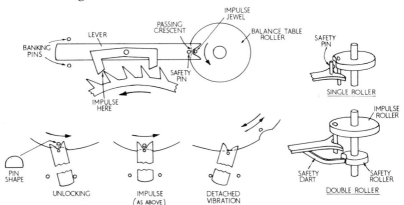

The English table-roller lever escapement.

Should the lever become displaced from the correct position when the balance is in the detached portion of the vibration the safety pin situated at the bottom of the lever slot will come into contact with, and rest upon, the outer surface of the balance roller. The frictional-rest safety action will continue until the roller jewel engages with the lever slot. The outer surface of the roller has a small passing crescent in its surface to allow the safety pin to pass during the normal unlocking and impulse action.

As an alternative to the safety pin and passing crescent on the single roller arrangement, two rollers may be used. The first, called the impulse roller, has the impulse jewel fitted and performs the escapement action. The second smaller-diameter safety roller with the passing crescent operates with a safety dart protruding from the underside of the lever rather than a safety pin. This is also shown in the figure above.

From 1850 onwards almost all the watches made in England used this design. In this form the escapement is long lasting and accurate and many watches initially fitted with other escapements were converted to detached lever late in their working lives.

Swiss Lever Escapement

The Swiss lever escapement shows a change in the layout and a change in the form of the escape wheel from all the other lever escapements discussed. The escapement is arranged so that the balance staff, lever shaft and escape-wheel shaft are in a straight line (shown opposite) rather than forming a right angle. The lifting and pivoting of the lever is caused partly by the shape of the lever pallets and partly by the shape of the escape-wheel teeth. These teeth have a sloping surface on a broad foot rather than coming to a point. The purpose of the change in shape is to divide the lift between lever and escape wheel which is now said to have club-tooth form.

The action of the escapement is the same as that described for the English table-roller lever. The Swiss form uses the double-roller arrangement with a safety dart protruding from the lower surface of the lever. Thus the swing of the balance allows the impulse jewel on the impulse roller to engage the lever slot, unlock the train and receive impulse. The balance then becomes detached whilst the lever is held to the banking pins by draw. Safety action by the dart resting on the safety

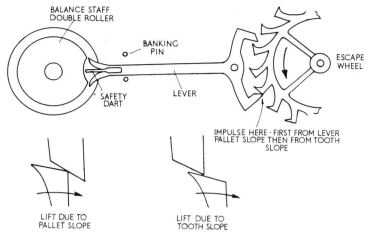

The Swiss lever escapement.

roller will occur should the lever move from the correct position.

The Swiss lever escapement is now the only mechanical escapement made in large numbers for high-quality watches.

Pin-lever Escapement

The pin-lever escapement, developed from the Roscopf design of 1867, is a cheap escapement for mass production. The original concept of producing a watch for the ordinary man has been overtaken by the mass production of jewelled Swiss lever escapements, but the pin-lever escapement is still the normal arrangement of the very cheap watch; it is the only alternative available to the Swiss lever (excluding electronic designs which do not use a balance-wheel arrangement).

In the pin-lever design the impulse pallets on the lever are replaced by steel pins. These pins perform the same duty as the jewelled pallets in that they allow the escape wheel to rotate in increments as they alternately unlock the train to receive impulse and lock it. The escape-wheel teeth supply most of the lift and have steeply sloped faces. This may be seen in the drawing (shown below). At the end of the lever the impulse is transmitted to the balance wheel by a forked end with a wide slot which engages with a metal impulse piece on the balance staff. Safety is by means of a dart operating on a roller with a passing crescent fitted to the balance staff. An alternative design uses a pin on the balance roller or balance arm to receive impulse.

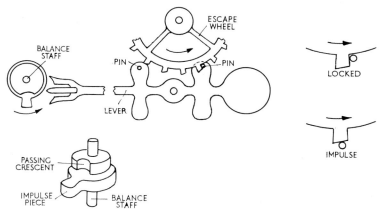

The pin lever escapement.

The Roscopf design used a right-angled layout, but pin-lever escapements are also made in straight-line form. Early pin-lever watches used a three-wheel train but later both three- and four-wheel trains were used so that the escape wheel may rotate in either direction and seconds hands may be used.

A consideration of timekeeping is now in order. In early watches time-keeping was poor but the application of the balance spring gave such an improvement that the disadvantages of the frictional rest escapements became obvious and a variety of other escapements were developed. The influence of the desire to navigate successfully has been mentioned in the historical survey and it was the spur to many makers. The knowledge that a detached escapement was essential to easily achieved accurate time keeping (although Harrison demonstrated accuracy with a frictional-rest design) led finally to the detent and the lever escapements. All good watches had one of these by 1850. The frictional-rest verge and cylinder escapements lasted much longer, but mainly for a market dominated by tradition or price; the verge tradition died over the succeeding twenty years and the cylinder was overtaken by cheap lever watches about seventy years later. So by 1925 the detached lever escapement had ousted all others — in basically two forms: the Swiss lever and the pin lever.

Accepting the detached escapement as a necessity, the problems to be met to achieve good timekeeping were dominated by the effects of temperature. Temperature change affects timekeeping in three ways. First, and most important, the balance-spring metal is less springy at high temperatures and more springy at low temperatures. Thus a watch will lose at higher temperatures and gain at lower temperatures. Secondly, temperature variation causes the balance to expand or contract. A hotter balance that has expanded.has its mass at a greater radius, and under the application of a constant torque will take longer to vibrate, so that a watch will again tend to lose at higher temperatures. Finally, expansion and contraction will affect the dimensions of the balance spring. Thus some form of temperature compensation is required.

Initial attempts at temperature compensation used bime- tallic curbs, made of two thin layers — one of brass and one of steel. When heated or cooled, the different rates of expansion of the two metals will cause the composite material to bend. One end of a curb is fixed whilst the other, the free end, is arranged so that it holds the balance spring close to its point of attachment to the watch plate. If the watch gets hotter and tends to slow down, the curb shortens the length of the balance spring and, it is hoped, speeds the watch enough to compensate for the loss. Curb compensation is an improvement over no compensation, but interfering with the balance spring is not an ideal way of tackling the problem. The shape of the end curves of a balance spring influences its isochronism, its ability to take the same time for a vibration irrespective of the arc of vibration; a curb compensating for temperature changes is liable to introduce other errors. A far better method was devised in which the balance rim was made of two different metals and then cut close to the balance arms (see drawing on page 27). The outer layer was made of brass and the inner layer of steel. When the balance temperature rises the higher coefficient of expansion of brass will cause the outer layer to lengthen more than the inner layer and the cut will allow the rim to bend inwards. Thus the balance mass will be moved inwards and the vibration time will be shorter. By carefully calculating the relative thickness of the brass and steel layers, the amount of compensation can be made appropriate to the loss expected due to the temperature rise. Similarly, if the watch becomes colder the balance rim will move outwards, compensating for the expected gain. The compensation obtained by this method is not exact, because the rate of variation of timekeeping due to change of elasticity with temperature is not always identical to the rate of variation of timekeeping due to change of balance dimensions with temperature. This may be examined mathematically and it is suggested in Chapter 3 that the mathematically inclined collector might find some interest in thinking about time-keeping. A simple graph may be used to illustrate the effect of these different rates of change and the diagram shows that it is possible for compensation with a cut-compensated balance to be correct at two temperatures where the two curves cross. In between these two ideal situations is a small middle-temperature error and in this area the watch will gain. Outside the two ideal situations the watch will lose. The effects of these errors can be minimised by manipulation of the mass and circumferential distribution of the compensation screws

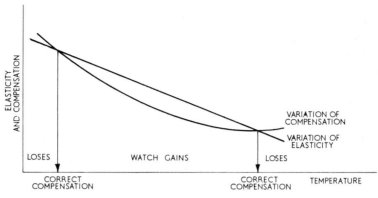

Middle temperature error.

around the rim. This is a skilled task, for not only is the compensation affected by altering the mass but so is the fundamental time of vibration of the watch. However there are also two timing screws available at the ends of the arms which will not affect compensation but which can be altered to give a basic change in mass or mass distribution. Any alterations in a balance must also be made in such a way that the poise of a balance is maintained, that is the centre of gravity is retained on the balance axis so that it does not have a 'heavy' side.

Middle-temperature error is a fact of life with the cut-compensated balance. There are numerous auxiliary compensations where additions to the balance are made in an attempt to limit excessive compensation, or to bring in extra mass when temperature changes are large but no perfect solution is found possible. These refinements are usually for use in the boxed marine chronometer and are rarely found in watches. An alternative approach to middle-temperature error is a metallurgical one. In the late nineteenth and early twentieth centuries, special nickel-iron alloys were developed by Guillaume. One of these was made so that when used in place of steel as the inner layer in a cut-compensated balance the compensation achieved was such that middle-temperature error was considerably reduced. Guillaume had also developed an alloy which did not expand or contract when subjected to changes in temperature. This alloy, known as Invar, has considerable possibilities for use as a balance material for it would eliminate the second error mentioned above. However the elasticity problems remain. Guillaume took his metallurgical work a stage further and worked out the correct alloying materials for a balance spring which would have no change of elasticity with temperature, and after some years of experiment Elinvar was successfully alloyed. Thus from 1919 it was possible to have a watch with Elinvar spring and Invar balance which should have minimal errors due to temperature change. These alloys had some disadvantages such as being prone to rust, difficult to work or susceptible to magnetic effects but following the Guillaume lead metallurgists have produced improved materials for use in watches. However, not all watches incorporate these advanced compensation techniques for many watch users are quite satisfied with the excellent performance of the non-chronometer watch.

Accuracy is affected by the rate of vibration of a watch. With a high-count train, that is one with a high rate of vibration, one faulty vibration will have less effect than with a low-count train. The count of a train may be obtained by multiplying the numbers of teeth on the centre, third, fourth and escape wheels together and dividing by the product of the numbers of teeth on the third-, fourth- and escape-wheel pinions. This will give the number of complete vibrations per hour, since it is based on one revolution of the centre wheel. The count is usually twice the number of complete vibrations, since there are two escapes per vibration on all but duplex and chronometer watches. Bearing in mind that the fourth wheel must rotate once per minute if it is to indicate seconds, there are a considerable number of combinations of teeth on these wheels and pinions which may be used in a train. A common modern count is 18,000 per hour which means that there are 5 escapes per second or 2.5 complete vibrations per second, older watches will exhibit lower counts — 14,400 per hour representing a watch beating quarter seconds is frequently used. The ultra-modern, quartz-crystal electronic watches with very high frequency vibrations have an inherently high capability for accuracy.

As accuracy increases in a watch, errors which were relatively small begin to assume a new significance. One such error is a result of position. A clock or chronometer is arranged so that it can be regulated to keep good time in one situation, but a pocket or wrist watch is required to give comparable accuracy regardless of position. A series of tests on a good watch in which temperature effects have been minimised and for which the temperature effects remaining are to be allowed for by a rate of loss or gain, will show that this rate varies slightly, depending on whether the watch is tested with the 3, 6, 9 or 12 figure on the dial uppermost.

One method of dealing with positional error is to arrange that the escapement rotates steadily so that the error is averaged and a single rate may then be used for the watch. This method is used in the tourbillon and the karrusel watches (both shown overleaf). In the tourbillon the escapement (balance, escape wheel, etc) is mounted on a carriage which carries a pinion driven by the third wheel. The fourth wheel is fixed and is concentric with the carriage shaft. The escape-wheel pinion meshes with the fixed fourth wheel. Thus, as the carriage rotates, the escape-wheel pinion will roll around the fixed fourth wheel which will cause the pinion to rotate and operate the escape wheel and balance in the normal way. The tourbillon was invented by Breguet in 1795 and in this design the mainspring power is transmitted to the escapement by the rotation of the carriage. In the karrusel watch, patented nearly a century later by Bonniksen, the carriage is mounted on a karrusel wheel driven by the third-wheel pinion. The fourth-wheel staff passes through the centre of the karrusel bearing to

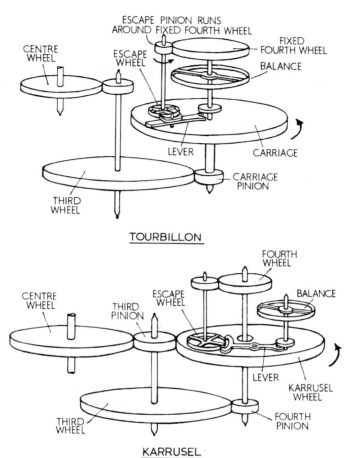

ESCAPE PINION RUNS
AROUND FIXED FOURTH WHEEL

FIXED
FOURTH WHEEL

CENTRE
WHEEL

ESCAPE
WHEEL

BALANCE

LEVER   CARRIAGE

CARRIAGE
PINION

THIRD
WHEEL

TOURBILLON

FOURTH
WHEEL

CENTRE
WHEEL

ESCAPE
WHEEL

BALANCE

THIRD
PINION

LEVER

KARRUSEL
WHEEL

THIRD
WHEEL

FOURTH
PINION

KARRUSEL

The principle of revolving escapements.

allow the fourth-wheel pinion to mesh with the third wheel and power is transmitted to the escapement in the normal way rather than through the carriage rotation as in the tourbillon. The rate of rotation of the karrusel is about once per hour compared with the tourbillon which may rotate once per minute. Both these designs require considerable skill to manufacture, and are only found in watches of high quality.

A watch is often required to do more than indicate time. The most common of the complex mechanisms to give extra information indicate date, day, month and moon state; then, chronograph watches have independent seconds hands capable of being started, stopped and returned to the start position whilst the mean-time hands continue to work normally. There are also watches which have repeating mechanisms which will, when activated, strike bell or gongs with a pattern that is recognised to give time to the last quarter hour, half quarter hour or minute.

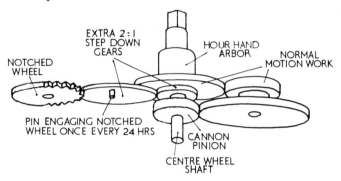

Date work.

Date, day, month and moon indication may be achieved by extending the motion work. The centre wheel rotates once per hour and the normal motion work is arranged to give a concentric rotation of the hour hand once every twelve hours. Day and date need to advance once every twenty-four hours so that a two-to-one step-down gear from the hour-hand drive will give a wheel rotating at the correct speed (drawing shown above). One method is to fit this wheel with a single pin which is used to move a notched wheel once per revolution. If a 31 notch wheel carrying an indicator or pointer is used the mechanism will show date but will need hand adjustment to allow for months without 31 days. A similar arrangement may be used with a 7-notch wheel to give days of the week. The month indication may be operated externally by hand or by a dial driven by a single pin from the 31-notch wheel. There must be an external adjuster to allow days of the week to be phased with the date. Very complex watches have been made with perpetual-calendar operation to allow for both variation in the length of the month and for leap-year variations. Moon indication from motion work is based on a 29½ day cycle using a 59 or 118 notch or tooth wheel.

The chronograph watch has three extra functions to perform: the starting, stopping and returning to the starting position of a seconds hand which is independent of the working of the watch. The starting and stopping is achieved quite simply by bringing a wheel (with extremely fine teeth or serrations) into mesh with another wheel which rotates permanently with the main train of the watch. The engaging and disengaging is achieved by pushing the winding button or a special button which operates a spring-controlled lever system. The lever ends not concerned with engaging or disengaging feel their way into, and out of, slots in a column wheel which rotates one step at each push of the button to control the stop, reset, start sequence. A third push on the button is used to reset the seconds hand. This is achieved by a special heart-shaped cam which is pivoted in such a way that when the heel of a spring-loaded piece presses against it, the torque will bring the cam around to the starting position. It is held in this position with no overshoot by the foot of the spring-loaded piece applying the pressure. The foot rests on a flat surface on the cam profile (drawing above right). The profile is such that if the watch is stopped before the seconds hand has completed half a revolution, it will return in an anticlockwise direction but if more than half a revolution has been made, the return is in the clockwise direction. The hand returns by the shortest route.

The repeating watch is required to sense the time and then make a sound on bell or gongs that conveys an indication of

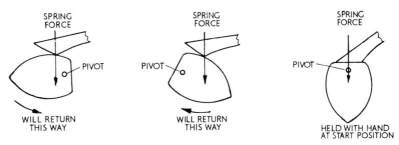

The chronograph reset mechanism.

time to the listener. As an example, consider a quarter repeater which strikes on one gong, 'ting', to indicate the last complete hour and on two gongs (one of which may be the hour gong), 'tang-ting', to indicate the last complete quarter hour. Thus, 'ting, ting, ting, tang-ting' means that the time lies between 3.15 and 3.30. The essential mechanism for producing this effect is quite straightforward but the under-dial work will look complex. The repeating mechanism has its own spring which is wound by pushing the pendant or moving a slide piece on the watch case. The push action also operates a curved rack which rotates a pinion attached to a wheel with 18 teeth. Twelve of these teeth are used to operate the hour strike-

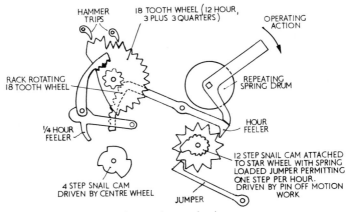

A repeating mechanism.

hammer and two sets of three for the quarter-hour hammers. The amount of rotation given to this wheel must be such that the hammers indicate the correct time. From the drawing it may be seen that this rotation is controlled by a twelve-step snail cam (one step for each hour), which is driven by the motion work, and a four-step snail cam (one for each quarter) attached to the centre-wheel shaft. The amount of rotation is determined by two feelers which abut on to the two snail cams. Thus when the repeat mechanism is actuated, the spring is wound and the time is sensed by the position that the 12 tooth/3 tooth/3 tooth wheel takes up. When the pendant or slide is released, the spring drives the toothed wheel round and each tooth trips the hammer as it passes it. For two sounds there are two trips. The speed with which the hours are sounded is controlled by the rate of rotation of a friction fly which consists of a ratchet and spring-loaded pawl.

There are other designs of repeating watch which use similar mechanisms. Many incorporate an all-or-nothing piece which ensures that the correct time is sounded by not releasing the mechanism until the pendant or slide is fully depressed. If it were not included a false time could be obtained by only partly pushing the pendant or slide. If this is done the all-or-nothing piece allows the repeating spring to unwind but sound no gongs.

Chapter 3
COLLECTING

The historical survey in Chapter 1 divided the period from the appearance of the watch to the present day into several separate fields. It is convenient to start considering collecting in these same groups. The first, which ends in 1600, is probably best regarded as a museum field. A collection of these watches is not feasible. The enthusiast will limit himself to seeing and, if possible, handling and photographing examples in museums and private collections. The second group, of the period 1600-75, are pre-balance spring watches and again are largely museum pieces. This was a period of decoration and the watches appeal to connoisseurs of enamelling and jewellery as well as to watch collectors; prices are relatively high. A 'puritan' watch in a plain oval case of blackened, tarnished silver, probably rather battered in appearance, might possibly be found, but with television, newspapers and books giving wide publicity to all antiques it becomes less likely. The very scarcity of watches of this age means that the majority of those surviving are already in museums or private collections.

The next period offers more hope. After the introduction of the balance spring in 1675 there was a period of experiment followed by fifty years of attractive, conservative design with decorated movements, champlevé dials, etc. These watches are still expensive, but after 1750 plain white-enamel-dialled watches in plain silver pair cases become quite common. Their prices require considerable thought before acceptance but are within the range of credibility. Thus collecting becomes viable

Two views of an English watch with cylinder escapement by Thomas Farr, Bristol, no 5316, in a silver case hallmarked 1815. The fusee has maintaining power, the balance is oversprung and a stop mechanism operates a bar which contacts the balance rim (missing). The movement is fitted with a dust cap.

from about 1750. The next group (1775-1830) offers possibilities, with a reasonable chance of a bargain. This is because the pair case disappears or becomes much less common towards the end of this period, and quite interesting watches are contained in unimpressive, single cases. Similarly, watches of the next two periods, 1830-1900 and 1900 onwards, may be found at prices dictated by the scrap value of the silver in the case. There are of course expensive watches in these periods: quality must influence the price. A brand-new wrist watch today can cost £3 or £300, say $7 or $700.

Prices are difficult to discuss except in the context of the amount of money that the collector is prepared to spend. Even in the groups that have been nonchalantly bypassed as museum or connoisseur fields there are a few people who will pay the enormous prices required. However, these are not ordinary collectors but investor collectors, who will seek expert advice from several sources before making a purchase. Such prudence is also necessary in the more humble price ranges inhabited by the ordinary collector. Unless a watch has such special significance that the cost becomes less relevant, the collector must carefully assess its value both on the open market and as an asset to his collection. He must satisfy himself of its genuine status and condition (Does the case belong to the movement? Is it in working order?), the likely repairs required, the possibility of finding another if he rejects it, the possibility of disposing of it if he finds a better example or gives up collecting in that period or style. At some stage in the price scale, different for each collector, the cost can be considered negligible enough for a watch to be bought as a speculative venture irrespective of the condition.

In the inflationary world prices change rapidly; those below are indicative of recent trends but without seeing the watches it is not possible for a reader to obtain an absolute assessment. It is also worth remembering that collections only have a money value when a customer is available, and in times of restriction prices may fall. A collector should not regard his collection as a gilt-edged investment.

Mean buying price	Spring 1970	Spring 1974
Plain silver pair-cased verge watch dated 1770	£25 ($60)	£75 ($180)
Plain silver pair-cased verge watch dated 1810	£10 ($24)	£30 ($72)
Plain mid-Victorian silver-cased lever watch	£1-£2 ($3-$5)	£3-£7 ($7-$17)

Study contemporary prices in watch dealers, auction rooms and antique, bric-à-brac and secondhand shops or stalls. The prices above are within the range of credibility mentioned earlier. To an investor the rise in price over the period might seem attractive, but to a collector it is depressing, since his chances of affording older watches steadily recedes.

In general, pair-case watches command a higher price than

Two views of an English watch with duplex escapement by Wm Thomas, Strand, in a silver hunter case hallmarked 1817. The fusee has maintaining power, the balance is oversprung and has a brass rim with three timing screws. The notched cylinder is of ruby. The movement has a dust cap.

single-case watches. They are usually older and are easily recognised as 'out of the ordinary' by the most uninformed owner; indeed they are often overpriced because of this. Similarly any form of decoration will increase the price since it is easily recognised by the layman. Silver cases are less expensive than gold, which are often completely outside the price range of the ordinary buyer. Gold prices have risen sharply in recent years; they may fall in the future but it is a good generalisation that the ordinary collector must avoid gold cases. Two similar watches were offered in early 1974 by one dealer, both late verges in single cases, not by eminent makers, perhaps 1840: the gold-cased watch, plain and attractive, was priced at £100 ($240), the silver-cased watch at £12 ($30). The movement in the gold watch was better looking, cleaner and more attractive than the almost identical one in the silver watch; it had a jewelled cock bearing. But if the gilding on the movement of the silver one was cleaned by the purchaser it would have been equally attractive.

If a watch comes from an eminent maker its price can be ten times that a similar item from a humbler craftsman. Thus the ordinary collector is unlikely to purchase watches by the greatest names but he should be aware of perhaps fifty good makers so that he can recognise a bargain when confronted with one. There is not always time to go away and think about it when you discover a Graham watch, but you must be sure that it is the right Graham and not a fake (unless the price is the correct one for an ordinary watchmaker's product).

Rather than embarking on haphazard, magpie-like collecting it is worth considering the possibilities within the 1775-1975 period in more detail. The 1775-1830 group enables the collector to acquire examples of each of the escapements described in Chapter 2 (except the mass-produced pin levers). These escapements represent the majority of those produced in any quantity in the life history of the watch. There are other, rare, escapements not discussed in Chapter 2 but these will be expensive. Of those listed, the verge and the table-roller English lever would be the easiest to find, but the remainder — with the exception of the detent — are obtainable at a reasonable price, given patience and a little luck. Provided the collector knows in what sort of case he is likely to find the particular escapement he seeks he may well be able to find what he wants and buy reasonably. However, if he asks for a specific, uncommon escapement he is bound to pay the prevailing price. To many dealers a watch is a watch unless it is in a pair case, when it is a verge. A collector with some expertise is in an advantageous position on some occasions. The most expensive watch in the common escapements of this period is the detent found in the pocket chronometer. This is likely to be outside the credible price range, but it might be possible to strike a collecting compromise and have a late-nineteenth-century example which will be more reasonably priced.

This group is at the expensive end of the range of viable prices. However, it is one of the more interesting because of the considerable variety available. Probably the best way of approaching the period is to start at the 1830 end and work backwards as experience and confidence increases or when a suitably priced earlier watch becomes available. It is important not to be over confident and it is probably wisest to study the various types of watch in museums, collections and illustrated literature before purchasing one. The table below has been included as an aid in this study. It may be seen that the style of a case may give an idea of what is to be expected

Two views of an early twentieth-century pocket chronometer, no 73602, by Maurice Dreyfus, Chaux des Fonds. The three-quarter plate watch has a helical balance spring, a pivoted detent escapement, a going barrel and a cut compensated balance. The hunter case is engine-tuned all over and the hands are adjusted by a rocking bar operated by a lever adjacent to the four-hour mark.

A chaffcutter (Debaufre type) escapement watch movement by Josh. Dumbell, Liverpool, no 817. The movement is in silver pair cases hallmarked 1825. The style shown by this view is closer to that of the lever but from the look of the watch, with a contrate wheel, it could be taken as a verge watch. The double saw-tooth escape wheel operates on a single pallet on the balance staff; there is a fusee without maintaining power but no dust cap.

inside and when the case is opened the style of the cock may give an idea of the type of escapement to be expected. Similarly it is advantageous to know the style of letters used in the hallmarks of the period at the London, Birmingham and Chester assay offices. The majority of watches of this period that are available will be English and will have been marked at these centres. Continental watches will not necessarily carry a hallmark but they are often identified by the bridge style of cock. If the watch has a maker's name and place of origin then it may be possible to find the maker listed in *Watchmakers and Clockmakers of the World,* G. H. Baillie (1963). This period is about the limit of usefulness of this book for the comprehensive listings stop at 1825. Only makers of particular significance are listed for later years. In this group, as in all collecting, the more watches handled the better and, because it might be possible to find something interesting at a reasonable price, the knowledge gained by study will enable the collector to avoid becoming visibly excited if his luck is in.

Watches 1775-1830

Escapement	Pair case	Single case	Cock	Recognition by	Plate on page
Verge	yes	rarer	round and pierced	contrate wheel	22, 23, 108
Cylinder	yes	after 1810	round and pierced, solid later	escape wheel teeth	83
Chaffcutter	yes	yes	round and pierced becoming lever shaped	contrate wheel	88
Rack lever	yes	rarer	special shape with words such as 'patent'	shape of lever	92
Massey lever	no	yes	lever shape with words such as 'patent'	balance staff roller	96
Savage lever	no	yes	bulbous lever shape	pins on balance staff roller	98
Duplex	yes	after 1810	bulbous lever shape	escape wheel teeth (single beat)	85
Detent (in pocket chrono-meter)	yes	after 1800	lever shape	balance, helical spring (single beat)	—
English lever	no	yes	lever shape with words such as 'detached'	balance staff roller	31, 113

Common movement faults in this period

Balance-staff top pivot broken, fusee chain broken, mainspring broken, fusee drive pawls worn and slipping, balance spring damage, watch out of beat, wear in balance jewels

Left to right: a late nineteenth-century watch, a barred movement from such a watch, and an early twentieth-century watch. Both watches are Swiss in origin and have mass-produced, going barrel-cylinder escapement movements. Such watches were made for a variety of markets and price ranges, with metal, silver, gold or enamelled cases and plain or decorated enamelled, silver or gold dials. The numerals on the dial of the right-hand watch show it was made for the Turkish market.

The 1830-1900 group will also offer a variety of escapements but only in the first few years of the period. After 1840 choice practically ceases. The possibilities of collection are therefore the variation in form and layout of the classic English lever, the development of winding varieties (although the early designs are rare), balance types — brass, gold, steel, compensated, etc — Swiss machine-made watches from 1840, variations in lever design, early pin levers, Geneva ladies or fob watches, etc. Each of these groups, with the exception of the winding types, will offer a choice of watches at the lower end of the price range. Gold, of course, must be avoided and the small fob watches often have attractive coloured dials and engraved cases which tend to raise their price above their horological interest. These watches which usually have cylinder movements are very often broken and it is worthwhile establishing the cost of a repair to the escapement before purchase.

American watches of this period are another interesting possibility to the collector. It is unlikely that any of the scarce watches of pre-1850 will be found for these early American watches were made in such small numbers. There is the possibility of sub-specialisation here within one company or in the series of companies which form the history of one company. A study of the American watches for sale in Britain shows that there are plenty of the Waltham group available in the hundred-year span of the complex of companies. A disadvantage of this field to the British collector is that research would be largely concentrated in America so that lengthy correspondence may be involved.

A possibility of collection over the span from 1775-1900 is to collect from one town, one maker or one year but this will require a great deal of patience and searching. It might also be tempting to buy watches which fit the collection even though they are overpriced or damaged beyond repair. It would need good decisions.

From 1900 onwards a collector might specialise in early wrist watches. Attention could be paid to the development of the well-known companies and the watches they produced. This should again be possible without enormous expense. Alternatively, in the pocket-watch field an attempt could be made to acquire examples of the variety of complex mechanisms available, repeating, chiming, moonwork, date and day, chronograph, stop, etc. There is a tremendous number of watches available in this period covering a wide range of prices and it should be possible to build an interesting collection without difficulty. Many of the watches will be obtainable at prices which can be regarded as small enough to provide essential experience even if they prove to be not so desirable as that experience accrues.

The majority of the plates in this book illustrate watches made between 1775 and 1900. These photographs are not of watches by famous makers which are kept in museums or in safes or bank vaults but of ordinary watches belonging to ordinary people who have allowed their possessions to be

Two views of rack-lever watches. The *left-hand* movement is by Thomas Savage, London, no 36806. It has adjustable bearings for the lever. The escape wheel is of steel and has 15 teeth. The cock is marked 'patent' and the 'Liverpool jewelling' is clearly seen. The watch has a stop piece, fusee with maintaining power and a dust cap. The cock shape is typical of a rack lever watch. The *right-hand* watch is by Rt Roskell, Liverpool, no 7550, in plain silver pair cases hallmarked 1812 or 1832. It has adjustable bearings for the lever and a large escape wheel of brass with 30 teeth as the watch has a three-wheel train with fusee. The cock is similar to that in the *left-hand* view. There is no jewelling and no dust cap.

photographed. They have almost all been purchased after 1970 and as far as is known within the price viability limits suggested earlier. Thus they represent what the ordinary collector can hope to find. There are other books available which show watches by famous makers with significant mechanical or horological features, or watches in superb cases of gold or enamel.

Where does one buy a watch? At specialist watch dealers, general antique dealers, bric-à-brac shops, junk shops, watchmakers and jewellers. There are also street markets, stalls in market halls and, finally, auction sales. Auctions require time for viewing and assessment of the state and value of the watch (which requires confidence and experience) as well as time for bidding. The bidding can often be made on a customer's behalf by the auctioneer, given written instructions by the customer on the limit of his bidding. If you buy at a non-specialist auction the watches will be largely 'as found', as will watches bought in markets and junk shops. However, if buying from a specialist watch dealer it may be possible to get a written statement about the watch. Buying from a specialist is bound to cost more, for he has had to seek out the watch, possibly have it put into good order and hold stock, which will tie up capital; but to purchase from the professional may be a safeguard against false purchases in the more expensive ranges. Another source of watches is exchange, both with dealers and friends. As a collection grows there are often too many of one type of watch or your field of interest shifts.

The problem of fakes may be disturbing. It is perhaps relatively unimportant in watches costing a few pounds but there comes a price when faking is worthwhile. Nobody is going to make an 'antique' verge watch in the 1800 style, because the cost of making it will exceed the sale price unless the watch is inscribed with a well-known maker's name. In this case the purchaser is likely to make sensible checks to establish the genuine age and not make an error. However, movements, dials and cases individually worth very little can be brought together and married to produce a watch which may be sold for say, £50 ($120). So a purchaser would do well to satisfy himself that all the parts belong together. The dial should fit snugly into the recess on the case and not be surrounded by an off-centre gap; the three-part hinge connecting movement, case back and glass bezel should match up. Often the dial, movement and case are numbered, so see if they match. The outer and inner cases should have the same maker's initials and the same hallmark (watches do exist with the marks one year apart). The style of case, dial and movement should match, although bear in mind that a 1770 verge watch could have been recased in 1840 by a relation of the original owner who wanted a more modern-looking case. It is also possible that the

original cases were damaged or even so badly worn that at least
the outer case had to be renewed. If the movement has been
professionally recased the fit will be perfect, which is unlikely
in a marriage. The married movement may show spare holes
in the dial plate when the original dial has been replaced, but
if the watch has an intermediate hinge ring between the dial
and the movement then these will not be visible. There may be
a filled-in winding hole in the back of the case because the
married movement has its fusee winding square in a slightly
different place. Wear marks on the cases will indicate if the
two cases have been together for a long time and if the bow has
been changed there should be different rubbings.

Movements are sometimes modernised. A duplex of 1810
may have broken in 1860 and the owner may have had the
escapement changed to a lever which would be considerably
easier to get repaired and more satisfactory as a watch. This
work is perfectly genuine and may be worth collecting; the
error here would be to assume the watch to be an early lever.

However much care is taken many collectors will find that
some of their watches are not exactly what they imagined them
to be at the time of purchase. This is not to suggest that they
have been fooled, or that there is a huge industry of putting
together parts to sell, but that repairs and replacements made
in good faith some considerable time ago by watchmakers are
not easy to detect. The watchmaker who recased or
modernised a watch in a crude fashion would not have
attracted a lot of custom. A watch that is 200 years old would
have to have led a very sheltered life to have survived without
some repair.

A collection of watches will represent an increasing
investment as time passes (not necessarily by inflation but
merely by increasing numbers), and it is worth looking at the
relevant clauses in the household insurance policy. The
collection may need special mention to be covered, especially if
arranged in some sort of display. Accidental damage due to

dropping, etc, should also be considered — repairs may be expensive.

For some collectors the acquisition of complete watches is unnecessary. An interest in the mechanical form of the watch rather than the complete instrument is a perfectly good reason for collecting, and in this situation the purchase of a quantity of gold or silver which hides the part of interest seems pointless. In the past, many movements have been removed (gently or roughly) from their precious-metal cases; the cases have been melted down and movements are often available at a fraction of the cost of the complete watch. The older the movement the rarer they become and the more decoration they exhibit. To many collectors the movement is more attractive than the watch, irrespective of the mechanical interest. Sometimes in the past, the only part of the movement retained in the scrapping process has been the balance cock. Cocks have even been 'faked' and used as jewellery. There is no excuse for anyone breaking up watches today, but unfortunately the practice continues and pocket-watch movements from single cases dating from 1830 onwards are still becoming available. Similarly wrist-watch movements can be acquired, and may be used as part of a collection. Dials could be collected, or hands, but these are less likely to be found as separate items.

Watch keys may be collected but this is a very limited field for the early and interesting varieties are rare. The individual key, perhaps enamelled in the same style as the watch, should of course remain with the watch but it is possible to find a lone survivor. Watch papers are interesting in their own right. These are small, roughly cut, circular pieces of paper inserted between the pair cases (or sometimes in the back of a double-bottom case), usually with the maker's, repairer's or seller's name and place of work printed on it but often containing other information. They are not common for they are easily lost or the original owner may have discarded the 'advertising'.

Two views of a Massey lever watch in a silver case hallmarked 1828. The maker may be T. Lamb but the style of the engraving suggests an owner and date. The roller on the balance staff is of the second Massey type with a jewel between two supports. The watch has 'Liverpool jewelling', fusee with maintaining power, a stop piece and a dust cap. The cock is marked 'patent'.

Watch chains with hanging ephemera (chatelaines) are sometimes found but are not common enough to enable a collection to be really viable. Seals on chains have their own following and are hardly vital to a watch although they could provide some evidence of the history of a particular watch.

The data available on every watch, movement, etc, in a collection should be recorded. A card-index system is useful. The watch or movement should be studied, researched and written up. In this way the collector learns more about watches and will be led to new and perhaps more-interesting discoveries. Only by drawing on the store of information in books, museums and collections can the collector become more knowledgeable himself and only he can correlate the information in the form relevant to his own collection. A watch acquired quite casually may have an interesting and traceable history or its maker may have unknown connections.

Most watches will have no traceable history or yield no new information but it is worth making some effort to follow up any promising lead. The card index should also record mechanical details, work done, etc, so that nothing is left to memory. Even the most simple work done is often forgotten and it may prove important later when more information or experience suggests further work on it.

Watch literature is important. Books and journals contemporary with the period of collection should be bought or borrowed, which is feasible enough from perhaps 1850 onwards, with some earlier sources being available. The use of libraries (public, reference, university, museum, polytechnic and institution) is essential and library research facilities such as copies of old documents, out of print books, etc, are usually available to the genuine enquirer. Reading about the methods used by old watchmakers helps understanding of the old watch and the contemporary difficulties of timekeeping, regulation, balance springs and balances may be better understood if studied in the original documents. The mathematically minded collector could reach a better understanding of the friction, forces and vibrations in a watch, which will explain the reasons for the success or failure of many innovations.

Photography might be used to 'collect' in normally unavailable fields. In particular it might be possible to obtain permission to photograph watches in museums and private collections. In less-elevated watch fields, without the need for approaching museums, etc, it might be possible to photograph quite ordinary watches in friends' collections or dealers' stock which cannot be purchased because they are not for sale or because of the sheer volume of varieties available. A collection representative of a period can consist of both watches and photographs.

The manufacture of a watch is perhaps the ultimate achievement of a mechanically minded collector. It involves the deployment of a variety of skills, including machining, fitting, gilding, casemaking and enamelling. It may only be suited to a collector possessing a workshop and sufficient skill of hand to justify the time involved, but the skills and some of the equipment may be obtained and used at evening classes in local schools of arts and crafts. The tools may be acquired as a separate collection, for many of them are specialised and obsolete; the repairer does not need them for modern factory-made watches. Chapter 4 lists most of the tools needed by amateur watch repairers and the bibliography to this chapter illustrates other specialist tools.

A Savage two-pin lever movement by Thos Sherwood, Leeds, no 1234. The date is about 1820. The style of the balance is similar to that of a verge watch but it is oversprung. The movement has a fusee with maintaining power and a dust cap.

There are many other possibilities for collections. Once a sustained interest in watches is obtained it is possible to find a niche within the pocket of the least wealthy enthusiast. In all the mass of suggestion and discussion of research, however, it is important that the simple collector is not deterred: it is not necessary to seek these specialisations for there is pleasure in finding and keeping a haphazard collection of watches simply because you like them. This is the most important aspect of collecting: the magpie instinct.

Chapter 4
REPAIRING

A watch may be found to be in any of several states. If it is not working, due to damage, such as bending or breakage of parts, missing parts, corrosion, etc, its value both in terms of money and as part of a collection may be considerably reduced; but it may be so old or so rare that it has more value in an unrestored condition than a restored one. It may be in what can be called ticking order: complete and working in a desultory and discontinuous way. This may be caused by excessive wear, dirt, minor damage, etc. A watch in working order may be expected to go continuously under reasonable conditions, but the timekeeping may be poor and unreliable. The watch may also be reluctant to go satisfactorily in all positions, working perfectly well on a desk when the dial is up but soon stopping when carried about in the pocket. Finally, a watch may be in good working order, or as good as the average watch in daily use; it can be used to tell the time as accurately as its inherent capabilities could ever allow. It is unrealistic to expect a verge watch to give the same performance as a late-Victorian lever watch. It is also unrealistic to expect a watch to give of the best unless it regularly receives expert attention.

A collector must decide whether he requires all the watches in his collection to work or whether they can remain as he finds them. There will be protagonists for both sides but it seems reasonable that, with the exception of those mentioned above as being so rare that restoration could be detrimental, a watch which is a device for telling the time should be able to work in some fashion. Assuming that the collector subscribes to this view he may take his watches to a watchmaker, but this often means waiting a long time for the work may involve making a missing part with time-consuming trial-and-error fitting. Also, a watchmaker is usually so busy with the regular maintenance and repair of modern watches that he has little time for investigating and repairing an antique watch. The repair could be very expensive and may exceed the value of the watch to the collector. Therefore, when a damaged watch is available the collector employing a watchmaker to do his repairs would be wise to get an estimate of the cost of restoration before he decides on purchase.

Many collectors choose to repair their watches themselves. This can be a much more interesting proposition as the work is an extremely time-consuming and absorbing hobby, bringing considerable satisfaction when a watch which may have been broken for a long period is finally brought to life. There are two distinct approaches: either as an amateur, or as a spare-time watchmaker. The latter approach will mean tackling the work in a professional way, purchasing all the equipment needed to restore or renew any part of any watch. The collector taking this approach may already have the necessary skills but if not he must teach himself or attend classes in watchmaking, silversmithing, enamelling, etc. He will also need to make a considerable investment in equipment. These subjects have their own literature. The collector is more likely to see himself as a sparetime watchmaker after some years of interest, and probably after some experience with the amateur approach discussed below. Eventually the professional will seriously consider making his own watch, preferably incorporating as many complex mechanisms as he can.

The amateur approach is to start with very limited aims, possibly twofold: firstly, to be able to restore the majority of one's watches to at least ticking, and preferably working, order so that they will run continuously in at least one position; and secondly to gain skill, confidence and experience so that more ambitious work can be attempted. Initially an amateur will not be capable of making new parts but he can use ingenuity and spare parts from other watches to solve problems. His lack of skill and equipment will mean that initially there will be watches that he will have to accept as not working, but as progress is made the problems that seemed insurmountable will become possible. Because of their size, wrist watches would be a poor field for him to tackle, except that he can gain experience inexpensively and spare parts for such modern watches are often readily available. One of the most important characteristics to develop is patience: many jobs take a very long time and the restoration of a badly damaged watch could spread over months.

The remainder of this chapter is concerned with this amateur approach, suggests tools, materials and rules, and finally describes some basic operations. Some of the suggestions will cause head shaking by professionals: however, it is clearly stated in the 'rules' that everything attempted should be capable of being undone without any permanent record appearing on the repaired watch. This means that no damage has been done and the work can be repeated in a more professional fashion when the skills have been learned. It should also be remembered that many of the watches are beyond economical repair by a watchmaker, so that the amateur is improving the watch as well as having the pleasure of the work.

SOME RULES FOR THE AMATEUR WATCH REPAIRER

1   Never do anything permanent. The watch should always be left so that it could be returned to its original state. Some time later a better way of repair may occur, skills may improve, more equipment may become available or the watch may turn out to be more desirable in the original unrestored state, being discovered to be unique or rare.

2   Never start to dismantle a watch with the mainspring wound. This is particularly important because the majority

of escapements will allow the watch to run at high speed as the balance staff is withdrawn. If this happens there is a good chance of damage. The mainspring should be let down.

3   Always study, and if necessary sketch or photograph, the original state before starting work. Never dismantle mechanisms that are not recognised and understood. Find out first what it is and how it works, then decide how to proceed.

4   Be careful of applying force unless the construction is well understood. Unscrewing a left-hand thread with the customary anticlockwise motion will result in breaking the head from the screw — a simple example of misapplied force.

5   Always work on a clean bench and put the microscopic parts away as they are removed.

6   Always make a new part rather than cut or drill an existing part. Cutting and drilling are irreversible. Some modern glues are very strong and parts may be glued into place rather than screwed. (Some modern glues are too strong.)

TOOLS AND MATERIALS

The lists below might be regarded as the minimum needed to make small repairs. They are not exhaustive and each individual will add items as they become necessary. One of the most difficult aspects of working on watch parts is the small sizes involved and tools and jigs will be required to enable some things to be done. These are devised as and when they are required, but it is useful to remember that all these jobs have been done before and information in books or from watchmakers is invaluable. The illustrations in books will be found very useful.

Tools

screwdrivers   pin vices
tweezers   knife

needle files   eyeglass
broaches (cutting and polishing)   Archimedean drill
boxwood movement stands   drills
small vice   micrometer
stake and punches   hammers
screwhead slotting file   dust covers
work bench   spirit lamp
swivel light

It should be noted that these are specialist tools which are
very small and may not be available from a local shop. The
suppliers mentioned in the appendix should be consulted.

Materials
small diameter brass and steel wire for pins, etc
benzine and ammonia for cleaning
lubricating oil
releasing oil
replacement glasses
replacement mainsprings
replacement staffs
glues (Araldite, shellac)
pegwood
Arkansas stone
fine emery paper, polishing powder
old watch movements and parts from all sources

Of all the tools that are available to the professional
watchmaker the two that the amateur will find most useful are
the lathe and the staking tool. It may be worth acquiring a
lathe should one become available at a reasonable price. The
work described below has all been done without a lathe but
some of the jobs might have been easier with one.
Alternatively, turns—a rudimentary form of lathe and a
professional watchmaker's tool—are adequate for many jobs.
Turns are not described here but are adequately covered in the
bibliography relevant to this chapter. A simple rotating device
can be made from a pin vice (with a chuck which will

accommodate up to $\frac{20}{1,000}$ in diameter parts) provided that the pin-vice handle is small enough to fit into the household electric drill. The drill need not be used as a power tool but may be turned by hand (or, if a suitable pulley is fitted, by bow as was an old lathe) to give rotary motion for polishing or filing. The drill bearings are probably not adequate for the small-diameter turning involved in watch work but there would be no loss in making a trial. The drill is best held in a proper support if this type of work is to be attempted but a simple screw clamp and shaped wood block would suffice for most operations.

The staking tool is an extremely useful extra for the amateur repairer and if one is available at a reasonable price will prove a sound investment. It can save much frustration, can give confidence against breakage and save the considerable amount of time needed to make a special jig or tool. Essentially, the staking tool comprises a rotating platform with a range of hole sizes and a set of punches. The tool has a vertical guide through which the selected punch is inserted. The guide holds the punch so that its centre is exactly in line with the hole in the stake. Thus there is no fear of breakage and no problem of lining up and holding the work and the punch. The staking tool is used for riveting, punching, staff removal, etc.

WORKING WITH WATCHES
A description of the methods used to correct a number of faults follows. All the methods are suited to amateurs and should not be regarded as the only way of tackling a job. All have been used and have been successful in their limited aim.

Putting into beat
Often a watch will tick unevenly and stop because the neutral mid-position of the balance vibration is not in line with the correct point of the engaging lever, crown wheel or escape wheel. The watch is *out of beat*. To set the watch in beat these points must be correctly lined up. A study of the action of the

various escapements in Chapter 2 will indicate the correct
position. For example, the mid-vibration position for the
balance of a table-roller lever watch is with the impulse jewel
in the centre of lever notch. Since the lever does not remain in
this position but is to one side or the other, some judgement is
required. This is true of all levers; special care will be needed
with a rack lever since there is positive engagement between
the balance staff and the lever.

The first step in adjusting the beat is to let the mainspring
down. This is described below and ensures that no accidents
can occur. The neutral position of the balance can now be
altered by unpinning the outer end of the balance spring from
the post on the plate and rotating the balance the required
amount in the appropriate direction. It may be necessary to
remove the cock to gain access to the pin securing the outer
end of the spring. If there is not enough spring available, or it
has been broken off, then adjustment may be gained at the
other end of the spring. Remove the balance and rotate the
split collet holding the inner end of the spring to provide
adjustment at the outer end. The collet is a friction fit on the
balance staff. Should this action be necessary it is likely that
the balance spring has been broken off short and this means
that once the watch is in beat it will gain. When making
adjustments to balance springs extreme care must be taken for
their shape is important in maintaining isochronous
performance. Once they are bent out of shape the rate of the
watch will vary especially if used in a variety of positions. (See
also 'Balance springs' below.)

Balance springs

If a balance spring is missing or damaged it should be replaced
with one of the appropriate strength and size. These may be
obtained from a watchmaker or from an old watch. The count
of the train (determined as indicated in Chapter 2) will be
required to give the strength and the diameter must fit the

regulator curb pins. After the new spring has been fitted to the collet in the correct manner shown in the drawing (given below) make sure that it is central and in the correct plane. The holding pin should have a flat side against the spring and should not protrude beyond the hole through the collet. Place the collet on the balance staff in such a position that the watch can be put into beat. Next, test the rate of the new spring. Grip the spring with a pair of tweezers at the point that the curb pins will hold and rest the pivot of the balance on a smooth surface such as a watchglass. Set the balance vibrating and count the vibrations. Minor adjustments are possible by the putting-into-beat methods described above, but if the count is obviously wrong then a different spring should be tried. The most likely counts to be found when adapting springs are 14,400 or 18,000 per hour between which there should be no confusion. If a spring cannot be found to give the correct rate, one that is too stiff should be chosen and the height carefully and evenly reduced by rubbing on ground glass covered with grinding paste. The spring should be held embedded in a cork.

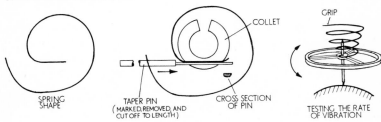

The balance spring.

   Balance springs are difficult to adjust accurately for all positions, temperatures, etc, and the amateur is unlikely to achieve perfect timekeeping without considerable experience. If the watch was not working but does after attention to the balance spring, then a big step has been taken and it is unwise to continue to seek perfection unless this is your particular interest.

Letting down a mainspring

In early verge watches the mainspring set up is by worm and wheel between the plates. A small key is required to fit the winding square on the end of the worm shaft, and the shaft is turned until there is no tension left in the chain connecting fusee and spring barrel. If the watch is fully wound this will require a considerable amount of turning.

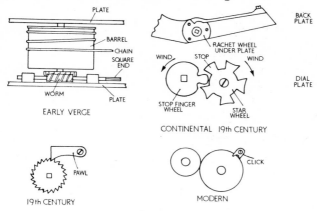

EARLY VERGE

CONTINENTAL 19th CENTURY

19th CENTURY

MODERN

Set up.

In later verge watches and English watches of the nineteenth century the set up is under the dial. Remove the dial (see 'Stripping a lever watch' below) and fit a key into the square protruding from the end of the ratchet wheel. Slacken the screw which holds the pawl tight. By initially tightening the spring the load can be taken from the pawl so that it can be pushed back with pegwood to free the rachet. Hold the key firmly so that the spring does not fly undone. If there is any danger of slipping, push the pawl back and perform the operation in increments. At the end of the letting down remove the loose ratchet wheel. Sometimes the amount of square protruding through the ratchet wheel is too short for this method, in which case let the ratchet off, tooth by tooth, using a screwdriver as a detent when the pawl is out of engagement. In continental key-

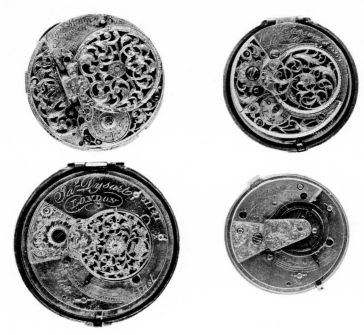

This group of four photographs shows the development of the verge watch movement from 1700 to 1850. All the watches have fusee and chain. The *upper left* movement by Cornelius Manley of Norwich, c1700, shows a large pierced cock with D-shaped foot and ears. The movement has Egyptian pillars and Tompion-style regulation with figure plate. The *upper right* movement by Wm Ransom of London is about 1760 and shows a smaller pierced cock with a smaller fan-shaped foot. The movement has square pillars and is thinner than that on the left. The *lower left* movement by Jas Dysart of London, c1820, is the largest movement shown. It has a solid foot to the cock and later Bosley-style regulation. The pillars are cylindrical. The *lower right* movement, smallest, c1845, has a bridge over the barrel for easy removal of the mainspring. The style of the cock resembles that of a lever watch of the period.

wind watches with a going barrel and barred movement there will be two places for attention when letting down the mainspring. Viewed from the back plate, the click keeping the spring wound is close to the winding square forming a V-shaped detent integral with, and on the end of, a leaf spring. This detent can be levered back and the spring allowed to unwind with the key held in the hand. Under the dial there will be a star wheel which is the stopwork fitted to limit the use of the spring to the middle portion only. Hold the lower (adjacent) square by the key and remove the star wheel. Holding the key in the hand allow the set up to unwind. Examine the action of the star wheel before removing it so that later it can be reset correctly with about threequarters of a turn of set up. It can be seen that one arm of the star has a convex end rather than a concave end and will not pass the stop. The number of complete rotations of the winding barrel is limited by the number of concave ends.

In modern watches and wrist watches the spring click holding the winding train can easily be seen above the top plate. The winding button is tensioned in the wind direction to remove the load from the click which is eased out of engagement with pegwood. The winding button must be held during this operation and then allowed to rotate slowly as the spring unwinds. It may be necessary to allow the click to re-engage and perform the letting down in increments.

There are other less common mainspring arrangements and careful attention to rule 3 in the list above is advised so that accidents are avoided.

Stripping a verge watch and reassembly

The movement must first be removed from the case by pushing out the hinge pin. This may be tapered and care should be taken to push in the right direction. If it is stuck apply a little releasing oil but it is not worth using undue force as the movement can be removed without disturbing this pin. To do this remove the hands and the dial (see below). The effect of removing the dial will be to release the movement from the case leaving the dial attached. The remainder of the operations are presented as a list. These instructions are for the older verge watch with complete unbroken top and bottom plates and worm set up between them. Later verge watches with a bar on the bottom plate, separate barrel cover on the top plate and rachet and pawl set up are stripped by the lever method which follows later.

Before starting to strip make sure that reassembly is possible. Put all the parts away as they are removed and label and make sketches as necessary. Try to avoid having parts of several different watches on the same bench.

1   Remove the hands using home-made levers or a puller. Protect the dial when using levers.

2   Remove the pins holding the dial or dial-backing ring from the bottom plate. There will be three feet protruding through the plate which are secured by pins. Beware of the motion work which may fall loose and get lost as the dial is removed. Lift the dial upwards off the movement to avoid this problem.

3   Remove the motion work.

4   Let down the mainspring. Support the movement on a boxwood stand whilst doing this.

5   Remove the balance cock, which is secured by a single screw.

6   Remove the taper pin holding the balance spring to the block on the plate. Remove balance-spring end from the block and the curb pins on the regulator.

7   Carefully lift out the balance complete with spring.

8   Remove the regulator mechanism and other decorative pieces from the plate.

9   Push out the four pins holding the plate to the pillars noting the position of the short pins.

10 Carefully lift off the top plate. The crown wheel will remain attached to the plate.

11 Remove wheels, barrel, fusee chain and fusee. The centre wheel will remain attached to the bottom plate.

12 If required, remove the crown wheel by pulling out the end bearing which is a taper fit.

13 If required, remove the centre wheel by removing the cannon pinion from the dial side of the bottom plate.

14 Check the action of the fusee stop piece (see drawing, page 121).

Reassembly is achieved by reversing the sequence of operations. The difficult step is replacing the top plate which must pass over the pivots of no less than five pieces. This must be done very carefully to avoid breaking a pivot. The watch is built up on a boxwood stand, and after the top plate is replaced assembly is straightforward. Lubricate the pivots of the watch but not the wheel teeth. Fit the balance so that the watch will be in beat. Test the running by applying a slight clockwise twisting force to the winding square of the fusee which simulates the mainspring action. The last part to be fitted to the movement is the fusee chain. Wind this on to the fusee by the normal winding mechanism and insert the hook at the end into the slit in the barrel (the barrel hook is the barbed one). Turn the set-up worm to apply tension to the chain and allow the watch to run until this set up is used up. Apply more set up and again allow the watch to run. Eventually the fusee chain will be on the barrel with the spring unwound. Finally, replace the motion work, dial and hands.

Stripping a lever watch and reassembly

Remove the movement from the case by pushing out the hinge pin in a similar way to that described for the verge watch. Some late levers may be held in place with screws with either half heads to be rotated free or whole heads to be removed completely. These types of movement pass out through the front of the case. If a button wind is fitted it must either be pulled back out of engagement or the small screw holding the stem in place slackened to allow the winding stem to be removed. The list of instructions below apply to the nine-teenth-century lever watch but with obvious adaptations they also apply to the late verge watch and to other nineteenth-century English watches with a variety of escapements.

1-7   Remove the hands, dial and motion work. Let down the mainspring. Remove the cock, the taper pin holding the balance spring and the balance. Detailed instructions for these operations are described above under 'Stripping a verge watch and re-assembly'. The watch should be on a boxwood stand.

8   Remove the barrel covering plate held by two screws. Never attempt to do this with the balance in place or with the mainspring wound.

9   Remove the barrel and the fusee chain if on the barrel. If the fusee chain hook is stuck in the fusee a little releasing oil may help. The set up rachet wheel from the back of the plate should have been removed when the mainspring was let down. If it was not it will now be loose.

10   Turn the watch over and remove the bar across the third wheel. This is held by two screws. Remove the third wheel.

11   Turn the watch over and remove the four pins holding the top plate to the pillars. Note where the short pins belong.

12   Turn the watch over. Carefully separate the plates leaving the wheels on the top plate on the stand. The centre wheel will come with the bottom plate.

13   Remove the wheels, fusee (and chain) and maintaining power detent. Remove the lever, which is partly underneath the balance bottom bearing.

14   If required, remove the centre wheel by removing the push-fit cannon pinion from the dial side of the bottom plate.

15   Check the action of the fusee stop piece (see drawing, page 121).

To re-assemble, reverse the operations. Place the top plate on the stand, insert the lever under the balance bottom bearing and between the banking pins, insert the escape wheel, fourth wheel, fusee and fusee detent. The dial plate with centre wheel is then placed on top and the only pivots to be fitted are the lever, the escape wheel and the fusee detent. Great care is still needed to avoid breaking a pivot. When inserted, turn the movement over on the stand (being careful to hold it together) and insert the four pins holding the top

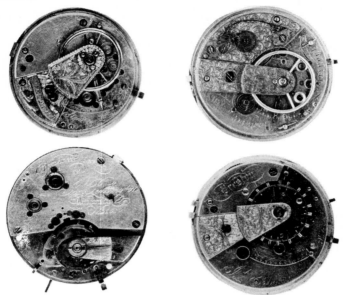

English lever movements of the period 1830-60. All the watches have a fusee with maintaining power. *Upper left:* a table-roller lever of about 1830 with deeply chiselled cock inscribed 'detach'd'. Maker unknown. It has 'Liverpool jewelling' and a big balance wheel overlapping the bridge over the barrel. *Upper right:* a decorated movement of about 1840 by Wm Roberts, Liverpool, which has the spring set up on the plate rather than under the dial. The arrangement of jewelling is further anti-clockwise than conventional because the escape wheel, fourth and third wheels are to the right of the lever (viewed from the top plate) rather than to the left. *Lower left:* a threequarter plate movement by Josh. Penlington, Liverpool, c1830, has auxiliary compensation on the balance to counteract middle temperature error. It is marked 'detach'd lever'. *Lower right:* movement by Josh. Blanchard, Preston, of the 1860 period when the style of the lever watch is fully developed. Of good quality with compensation balance and fully jewelled except for the lever pivots. The lever is curved-sided whereas the three earlier movements have straight-sided levers. The cock has minimal decoration.

plate to the pillars. Again reverse the movement on the stand, replace the fourth wheel in its pivot as it will have fallen out with the reversals, insert the third wheel and fit the bar across the plate supporting the fusee, third and fourth wheel pivots. Reverse the movement on the stand and replace the barrel and barrel plate. Lubricate the pivots of the watch but not the wheel teeth.

The chain of a lever watch can be put back before the balance is fitted. This avoids the chance of damaging the balance, but the chain cannot be put back at this stage in any other escapement. In the lever watch the chain is wound on to the barrel using the square protruding from the dial plate underside: hold the movement so that the barrel arbor is horizontal and allow the chain to run under a finger which keeps a small pull on the chain. If the chain is slack it may slip off the barrel and jam on the arbor. If this happens, remove the barrel plate and barrel, then the chain, and start again. Pulling at the chain may break it. When the chain is on the barrel, continue to use the finger to hold it and hook the free end to the fusee. Place the ratchet wheel on to the square and apply set up to put the chain in tension. Push the pawl into the ratchet with pegwood and tighten the pawl screw. Replace the balance and pin it so that the watch is in beat. Make sure that the impulse jewel is on the correct side of the lever jaws or the train will be locked. Replace the cock. The running can be tested immediately as the chain is already in tension under the set up. Finally replace the motion work, dial and hands.

In the late verge watch, and other escapements except the lever, the balance and cock must be replaced before the chain is put in. In these cases test the running by applying a small clockwise torque to the fusee winding square which simulates the mainspring action. Then wind the chain on to the fusee using the normal winding mechanism and gradually work it back on to the barrel by applying small amounts of set up. This technique is described under 'Stripping a verge watch and reassembly' above. If the watch has a dust cover this should be fitted when applying the small increments of set up; it will protect the balance.

Stripping and reassembly of other escapements

Watches with escapements other than verge or lever will usually be of similar construction to the early verge or the lever. Thus the techniques above may be used. The most important points are to make sure that the mainspring is let down before removing the balance and similarly not to apply any spring tension until the balance is replaced. Pocket chronometers, unrecognised escapements, tourbillons, karrusels, etc, should not be disturbed by the amateur.

There will also be watches that are assembled in different ways. The half-plate design is an obvious case. These may be taken apart carefully without damage, provided that the basic methods above are used.

In keywind watches with the set hands square on the back plate, both the centre wheel and the cannon pinion are push fitted to the arbor. The arbor is removed complete with the set hands square from the back plate after removing the hands, dial and cannon pinion.

Cleaning a watch

When a watch has been taken apart it may be cleaned by immersing it in benzine. However, the mainspring in the barrel, the balance and the lever should not be immersed but should be brushed clean with benzine. Prolonged immersion could disturb jewel settings. Do not be tempted to use petrol or any other solvent. Benzine immersion degreases the parts, which should then be brushed clean and dry. Holes and jewels should be cleaned out with pieces of pegwood. Pinion and wheel teeth may also be pegged clean if covered with dirt. Benzine treatment should bring the whole watch to a satisfactory state, but if the gilding on plates and wheels is not good enough it may be cleaned with a *weak* solution of ammonia applied by a soft brush and washed off with water. Thorough drying is essential to avoid rust in the future. The ammonia treatment should be tested on a spare part from another watch to judge the strength and result.

Pivots may be polished by using a polishing powder in a hole in the end of a piece of pegwood. This method will not repair damage but merely buff up the pivot which should afterwards be washed off in benzine; this is a treatment of dubious merit which could result in breaking a pivot, and in general, unless pivots show bad blemishes, they should be left alone.

After a watch has been cleaned the parts should only be touched at their edges or held in tissue paper. This avoids transferring grease or perspiration to the parts. However, a fingerprint is preferable to a dropped watch and discretion should be used.

Lubrication

Only the pivots of a watch train and escapement need to be lubricated. The wheel teeth should not be treated with any oil. The oil should be applied with a fine wire dropper to the reservoirs in the plates (or in early watches to the pivot point). Only the smallest amount should be put on the dropper to avoid drips in the wrong place, and anyway excess oil will spread to the wrong places. Also, dust will stick to oil and form abrasive mixtures. A good-quality oil should be chosen and the container should be kept tightly closed as the action of the atmosphere is harmful.

Strictly speaking, different grades of oil should be used on train and balance pivots, but for the collector whose watches are not going to run continuously a single grade may be chosen. Similarly in a lever watch the pallets should have a microscopic amount of lubrication, but for the collector it is better to keep oil from this area. The watch is not going to run continuously and some modern watches do not use pallet lubrication at all. The impulse jewel in a lever watch should not be lubricated. Oil is, however, required in the spring barrel. The surface of the spring should be coated to avoid rust and the top and bottom of the inner barrel surface on which the spring rubs needs lubrication.

Checking for faults

If a watch will not tick or show any signs of motion, and there is no obvious damage, it should be carefully stripped and cleaned. The train pivots should be examined for damage and

A view of a lever watch with fusee showing the conventional layout of the train. Balance and balance staff have been removed.

any really bad pivots straightened, cleaned, polished or renewed (see below). The holes in the plates should be pegged out and examined for damage. Really bad holes should be cleaned up with a polishing broach and extreme cases may be bushed. Unless accurate timekeeping is the aim it should suffice to clean up the holes rather than rebush in cases of moderate wear. Bent or damaged wheels should be straightened or renewed (see below). Check the action of the fusee to see that the power is being transmitted. It has been assumed that a broken mainspring is not the cause of the trouble, but the barrel cover should be removed to examine the state of the spring and to see that it is correctly attached at either end.

Reassemble the train without the fusee chain and without the escapement (balance or balance and lever), then apply a clockwise torque to the fusee winding square to simulate the mainspring action. The train should run freely. If it does not, there is an undetected fault. When satisfactory, fit the balance so that the watch is in beat; then again apply clockwise torque to the winding square. The watch should run. If not, there is a fault in the escapement to be detected.

In the case of the lever watch, the fusee chain may be replaced before the balance is fitted. It will have been necessary to take the train to pieces to insert the lever but when the chain is tensioned the action of the lever may be examined. When the lever is given a small displacement from the banking pin (by pushing the *fork* end across) and then released the draw should snap the lever back to the banking pin. When given a larger displacement to unlock the train, the lever should snap over to the other banking pin. This action can be tested for a complete revolution of the escape wheel, ie 30 escapes for a 15 tooth wheel. Provided this action is satisfactory the watch should work once the balance is fitted.

Mainspring replacement

The mainspring may be inspected after the barrel has been removed from the watch. To do this prise off the lid with a lever. If the spring is broken a new one identical in height and thickness to the original, should be obtained from a watchmaker. The length of the new spring should be such that when it is in the barrel it occupies half the space available. This is shown in the drawing. If it is too long it must be shortened and

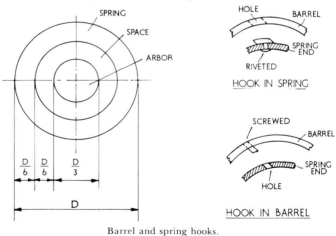

Barrel and spring hooks.

the new end softened by heating until red hot and then allowed to cool. A new hook and/or hole will be required at the outer end. If a hook was fitted then a new one must be filed from a piece of steel to suit the hole in the barrel. It must be made on the slant as indicated in the drawing and then cut off and riveted to the spring through the new hole drilled in the end. If the spring is fitted to a hook attached to the barrel the new hole in the spring must be cut at an angle in circular or rectangular form to mate with the barrel hook. This is also shown in the drawing. The state of the barrel hook should be examined in case it was the cause of the spring break. If it is worn, a new hook is made from a finely threaded steel wire and screwed into the barrel at the correct angle. If this is not possible with limited tools then an old hole may be found on the barrel which can be broached out and a spring hook made to fit.

A new spring should be fitted using a spring winder. The amateur is unlikely to possess one and unless a watchmaker will fit the spring he will wind the new spring in by hand. This is adequate for working watches but could give erratic timekeeping. The hand-winding produces a spring which is, when free, slightly helical in form rather than a true spiral. This gives a component of force acting against the barrel lid which tends to open it. If the lid is a poor fit it may open and jam against the plate. This is unlikely but the opening force will cause considerable friction between the spring and the barrel resulting in poor timekeeping. When the new spring is tested it may be found that the central hook on the arbor is not engaging with the hole in the spring. The spring centre should be bent gently inwards so that engagement is assured.

Repairing or cleaning a fusee chain

Fusee chains are often found to be broken but provided both parts are sound they may be repaired. The chain should be soaked in benzine or releasing oil and then wiped clean. A close examination should then be made to make sure that the repair is worthwhile. Large amounts of rust would make repair pointless for breakage would occur again but it may be possible to remove a faulty section.

A small punch is required which may be made from a needle

first softened or annealed by heating and then cooled slowly. The end should then be filed to the correct size and the needle hardened by heating to red heat and plunging into water, alternatively an old staff may be adapted using the pivot as a punch. The broken ends of the chain are stuck in turn to a riveting stake with Sellotape so that the rivet to be removed is over a hole in the stake. The punch is used to produce male and female parts. These are then brought together over the hole in the stake. A new rivet is made from an annealed needle or steel pin by filing the end to the correct size. This is inserted firmly and the excess length removed from both sides with a thin file such as a screw-head slotting file. The chain is replaced on the stake but not over a hole and the ends of the new rivet are peened over with a punch to stop it falling out. The watchmaker's eyeglass will be required for most of these operations.

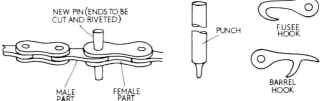

Fusee chain and hooks.

Should either hook from the chain be missing a new one may be made from thin steel. The hole should be drilled (and if necessary broached) first and then the hook filed to shape. The shape can be seen in the drawing, or another chain may be used as a pattern.

When the chain is deemed satisfactory by repair or if it was not broken but merely required cleaning, it should be given a thorough soaking in oil. An overnight period is not too long. Then run the chain backwards and forwards over a groove in a smooth, rounded corner of wood, at the same time applying oil liberally so that all the chain joints are free and lubricated. Finally, wipe the chain clean with a benzine-soaked cloth.

Repairing a fusee click

If the fusee rotates in the winding direction satisfactorily but fails to lock so that the spring tension immediately takes the chain back on to the barrel it is likely that the fusee clicks are worn or broken. The fusee is shown in the drawing given below. To strip the fusee, place the cone end in a boxwood stand and push out the pin passing through the shaft and the blued-steel washer. Lift off the washer. The fusee may then be separated into the great wheel of brass, the maintaining-power ratchet wheel of steel with the two clicks or pawls and the fusee cone with the driven ratchet wheel pinned to it. The clicks operate on this wheel and examination will show if it is wear or breakage causing the slip. If it is merely rounding off of the click points, these may be filed or stoned to give satisfactory working, but excess wear or breakage will require a new click to be filed from steel. In extreme cases the brass wheel with which the clicks engage may need some attention, but damage can usually be dressed out with a file.

It is possible that the damage may not be confined to the

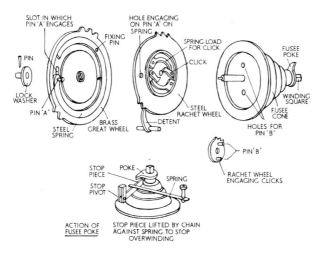

The maintaining power fusee.

clicks but may also include the spring pushing the click into engagement. In this case the fusee may be persuaded to operate with only one click; but it is better to file a new spring piece from steel. Both the clicks and the spring are secured by pins filed integral with the parts and peened over on the underside of the maintaining-power ratchet wheel. When the fusee is assembled with the new parts the action should be tested before pushing the pin back through the blued-steel washer.

The older type of fusee without maintaining power has similar clicks in the construction which will cause slipping when worn. Repair is effected by similar methods.

In the event of a fusee being missing or damaged beyond repair it may be possible to transfer one from another watch. The fusee must have the correct diameter and tooth spacing to mesh with the centre-wheel pinion. Differences in height can be accommodated by using a spacing bush to reduce end shake to an acceptable amount, provided the fusee stop and maintaining power detent will still engage.

Broken staff repairs

When pivots are broken on staffs that are difficult to replace or too expensive to be economically made, it is possible to replace half a staff by using the hub of the wheel on the staff as a joining sleeve. The drawing shows the principle involved. This method is more useful if the broken pivot is not on the pinion half of the staff but even on this half it is possible to wait until a suitable pinion with a good pivot is obtained before the repair is made. An alternative method is suggested below for pinion ends. Staffs are removed from wheels, levers, etc, by using a punch and a stake. The punch must have a suitable diameter hole to go over a pivot and deliver the blow to the shoulder of the staff. Many staffs have a taper and can only be removed in one direction. The dimensions should be checked with a micrometer to be certain of the correct removal direction. The height of the wheel on the staff should also be measured to

make sure that it is correctly replaced. If a replacement-part
staff is found on which the pivot is of the correct diameter the
staff diameter may be reduced by careful filing if too large, or

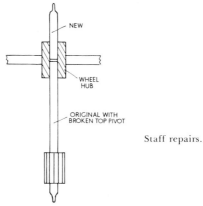

NEW

WHEEL
HUB

ORIGINAL WITH
BROKEN TOP PIVOT

Staff repairs.

set in with a non-permanent glue if too small. Always modify
the replacement part rather than the wheel hub or the pivot
hole in the plate. Obviously the total height of the composite
staff must be correct.

Verge top pivot, bottom pivot, verge and crown wheel
The top pivot of the verge may be repaired in a similar fashion
to the broken staff. It may be found that there is very little
room for this technique as the verge pivot is close to the
balance. In this case the brass boss on which the balance is
fitted and the broken staff may be bored out to allow a new
piece of staff to be fitted. This may be done with a hollow
cutter which removes the soft brass and allows the thin steel of
the verge to be broken off. The drawing below shows the
sequence of events in this repair. An alternative is to remove
the balance, file away half the thickness of the balance from
the boss and broken verge and bond on a new piece of staff.
This method is not as satisfactory as the first but is
considerably easier to achieve. In either method great care
must be taken to avoid damage to the rest of the verge.

If the bottom pivot is broken the correct method is to make a new verge. This can be done with a file but is a lengthy process with a chance of breaking the new part at a late stage. If the broken pivot is to hand it is possible with great patience and several tries to bond the pivot back into place with Araldite or some similar immensely strong adhesive. This technique may also be used with the top pivot. The result may not be satisfactory for permanent running but it is a method of producing a ticking or working-order verge watch. It may also be used with a replacement pivot but is more difficult because the broken staff and new pivot do not 'key' together.

If the verge is broken between the pallets or the crown-wheel staff outer-end pivot is broken off, a thin piece of bushing tube may be used to join the two halves or in the latter case to join the crown-wheel end to a new outer-end piece. There is very little room in this area for bulky extras and Araldite may be needed to add strength. The inner pivot on the crown wheel presents a different problem which may be solved by using Araldite to bond on a new pivot. An alternative is to use the method which is suggested below.

New pivot on the pinion end of a staff
If the pivot at the pinion end of a staff is broken and it is desirable or essential that the original pinion be retained, there may well be a problem. If there is sufficient length and room a new pivot can be bushed on to the old staff as in the case of the verge above. However there is often no room for a bush, for example, at the inner end of the crown-wheel staff in a verge watch. In this case the only alternatives which retain the original pinion are bonding with Araldite or drilling out.

Success with Araldite has meant that the drilling method has not been personally tested. In principle, however, a new pivot could be let into the pinion end of a staff if, after softening and filing off the broken parts flush with pinion face, a hole were drilled. Much will depend on the pinion core-diameter but with a reasonable diameter available it is

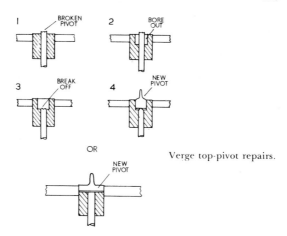

Verge top-pivot repairs.

well worth trying if no other method can make the watch tick. The author has seen it done by a professional repairer, and in this context it should be borne in mind that there are watches for which it is worth paying a professional to do such difficult tasks. Here it is assumed that the collector has a watch of little value for which he is seeking a method of repair that will give him satisfaction. A lathe would make drilling out a realistic proposition.

Straightening wheels, shafts and pivots

If a wheel is bent, it may be straightened by pressing between two flat surfaces. Some heat may be applied to the surfaces to ease the flexing. After this process it is likely that there will still be a kink at any point where the original bend was particularly sharp and this may be removed by light taps with a small punch. The teeth should not be hit lest they spread and interfere with meshing. If the wheel is broken as well as bent it may be soldered at the fracture. The repaired wheel should be put into its pivots and examined for truth and then tested with its pinion and any tight spots eased. If any teeth are missing a new piece of brass can be let into the rim of the wheel and soldered. Fresh teeth are filed to give satisfactory meshing.

Shafts may be straightened by tapping with the pane of a small hammer (or a similar-shaped piece of metal) on the concave side. If the high convex side is hit, damage is likely to occur. Heat applied to the anvil which will penetrate the shaft may help the process. Pivots can sometimes be straightened. When the pivot has been softened the straightening should be attempted in small increments. There is a good chance of the pivot breaking but if the watch did not work in the first place because of the bent pivot there has been no loss. In both shaft and pivot straightening operations there is no point in perfection with the risk of damage if the collector is satisfied with a nearly straight part which will allow the watch to tick. As soon as this is thought possible the train should be assembled and tested.

New wheels

If a wheel is so badly damaged that repair is impossible, or if a wheel is completely missing, it is possible to transfer a suitable replacement from another movement. The number of teeth and diameter is known or can be calculated by counting the teeth and measuring the size of the meshing pinion and the distance between the two shafts. The correct meshing of teeth is important but if it is a case of making a watch go, then trial and error can be used. If a wheel appears to be a satisfactory substitute it should be mounted on the staff and a trial made with the appropriate pinion. If the wheel is too small it may be possible to spread the teeth outwards by tapping with a hammer. The tooth sides will probably need easing with a file after this treatment. If the wheel is too large the diameter may be reduced with a file. Again the tooth sides may need easing. All modifications should be made to the replacement wheel, not the correct watch pinion, so that in the event of failure the watch is still intact and a fresh start can be made. Once the wheel runs satisfactorily with its pinion, the train should be assembled and tested before the whole watch is rebuilt.

If it is an escape wheel that is missing then the problem is more difficult. With cylinder, duplex or detent escapement the task is one for a professional antique watch repairer. The amateur should be able to make or adapt a crown wheel for a verge watch. A careful examination of a complete verge escapement will make the scope of the work clear and the bibliography for Chapter 4 contains books giving full details. This is a task for patient filing. With a lever watch it might be possible to take the escape wheel from a scrap movement and fit this in the damaged watch, but if an escape wheel of the correct size cannot be found then both the escape wheel and the lever may be planted in the damaged watch. The lever may need some adapting at the fork end. This transfer should only be attempted in a watch of little value for new pivot holes will have to be drilled in the plates to accommodate the new escapement. This is an irreversible step. This technique was used by professional watchmakers in the latter part of the nineteenth century when cylinder or duplex watches had their escapements changed to lever but has not been personally tested.

Filing out new parts

The file should never be underestimated. Provided that the work can be held in some way or a jig made to support it, and provided that adequate patience and time are available, a considerable range of replacement parts can be filed out. Bearing in mind that the conversion of a broken watch to a ticking watch is a considerable achievement, the fact that a part made by amateur hand-filing may leave much to be desired in timekeeping or continuous reliable running is trivial. As experience is gained, hand-made parts will improve in quality and it may be possible to return and improve earlier work. Parts the author has made in this way are a seven-tooth pinion, hands, clicks, hinges, etc, and parts made by other collectors include balance wheels, cocks, staffs, a verge-

bearing bracket, verge, etc. When confronted with a
seemingly impossible task, consider the possibilities of a file.

Bushing

If the pivot holes in a plate are so badly worn that bushing is
required then a decision has to be made. Bushing will require
holes in the plate to be enlarged, which is an irreversible step.
If the watch is of no great value then bushing can be attempted
without fear. The bushes can be purchased from a
watchmaker and come with an extended piece which can be
broken off after the bush is fitted. The old hole will need to be
broached out to give a good tight fit on the bush. Bushing
should be regarded as a habit to be avoided unless absolutely
necessary.

An alternative bad practice which is sometimes in evidence
on watches is to spread the metal around the pivot hole by
using a punch around the perimeter. The hole is then
broached to size. This again is a habit to be avoided but it
cannot be denied that it may achieve some success.

Pivot holes which are jewelled may also need repair.
Replacement jewels are available from a watchmaker but the
design is different from the jewels which were set in with
screws. If the original jewel is complete but damaged it is
possible to effect a repair with Araldite which will enable the
watch to run. It is also possible to transfer period jewels from
an old movement.

Impulse jewels

These are sometimes found broken in an otherwise perfect
lever watch. If a replacement jewel is not available then a
piece of steel wire may be used. The pin or jewel is not
normally circular but ellipse or D-shaped as shown in the
drawing on page 68. The D-shape is the easier to form, but
the hole in the roller should be the guide to the shape required.
The D should be formed by removing one-third of the circular
profile leaving a flat surface. Some early lever watches appear

to have been fitted with circular jewels and watches certainly function quite adequately with such jewels.

The replacement pin should be a sliding fit in the hole in the roller and the length just adequate to operate the lever without fouling the bottom pivot. The hole in the roller is filled with a non-permanent glue (shellac, varnish, etc). The new pin is introduced and adjusted and then the whole system put aside so that the glue sets.

Motion work

It is disappointing to find all, or part of, the motion work missing from an otherwise complete watch but it is not an uncommon fault. If one wheel only is missing it is possible to find a correct replacement in an old movement. The teeth numbers should be such that when combined with the two remaining wheels a 12 to 1 gear ratio is obtained. The diameter of the missing wheel must also be correct. The wheel centre may need broaching out to fit the pin or the cannon pinion on which it revolves.

In the absence of a suitable matching wheel it is better to take a complete set of motion work from another watch movement. This may require one hole to be made in the underside of the dial plate to take the pin on which the idler wheel rotates. It may also be necessary to broach out (having first softened) the centre of the replacement cannon pinion. The parts removed should be retained so that when a suitable matching wheel is found they can be replaced.

Hands

Replacement hands are available from watchmakers but they will be modern, pressed-out hands suitable only for post-1800 watches. Older hands such as beetle and poker designs were hand-filed from steel and this is how replacements should be made. First, drill the holes through the hands and broach or file the centre to the correct square or round size. Then file the hands to shape. These designs are not simple one-plane affairs but are contoured in two dimensions. A contemporary pair of hands should be used as a pattern. Finally, polish, degrease (with benzine) and then blue the hands.

Blueing

Steel screws, hands, springs, etc, are usually blued in pocket watches. To achieve successful blueing, polish and degrease the parts in benzine. They must not then be touched by hand. Place the parts on a tray and heat the tray with a spirit lamp. The heating will cause the polished steel to change through a range of colours passing through pale straw, dark straw, brown-yellow, yellow-purple, purple, dark blue, pale blue until the steel is finally colourless. The technique of blueing is to stop the process, so that the steel remains a dark blue with perhaps a tinge of purple. One of the main problems is to obtain a uniform colour which means a uniform temperature. If the tray is filled with brass filings and tapped during the process, it facilitates the even distribution of heat. It is also possible to use a heated metal block for thin objects and to slide the part about to achieve the uniform colouring.

If the result is not satisfactory the part can be made colourless by re-polishing and the process repeated. Acids can also be used to remove blueing and if a modern acidic agent is used to remove or inhibit rust on a blued part it will emerge colourless requiring reblueing. Acid treatments should be avoided.

Araldite

Araldite is the proprietary name of a two-component adhesive which is exceedingly strong when set. At room temperature the setting time is quite long but it can be shortened considerably by placing the bonded parts on a radiator. There is also a rapid-setting variety. Thus it is a very useful material and may be used to repair parts which would otherwise need to be replaced. Examples of its use are the bonding together of a shaft and pivot, the repair of a broken wheel, the repair of jewels and casework repairs. Because of its great strength it is not always possible to rebreak a part that has been joined with Araldite. This would not be true in the case of a pivot where the area for bonding is very small but if there is a large area then an Araldite repair should be regarded as permanent and it should only be used in situations where a permanent joint is required.

Case work

The amateur cannot afford to work on gold cases, for the new material is too expensive. Even silver is surprisingly costly when purchased 'new'. The silver used in watch cases is not pure but is alloyed with 75 parts per 1,000 of copper. However, the use of silver from scrap cases and case parts reduces the cost and may be chosen to be of the correct antiquity.

Silver soldering requires either a butane blow-lamp or mouth blowing from ordinary gas. Care must be taken to avoid melting adjacent joints and the lowest-melting-point solder available should be chosen. Wet rags placed on adjacent joints help to keep them cool. Parts to be soldered should be clean and grease-free and the correct flux should be used. Borax crushed in water is the usual material.

New pendants etc, can be cast from old case metal but the melting temperature of the silver is just too high for the small butane lamp and a large torch or kiln is better. New bezels can be made from silver strip but considerable skill is required to get satisfaction. New backs can be adapted from old cases. The best way to takle the problems of major casework is to attend a jewellery class at a local school of art and craft. They will charge for the course and for the materials used, but the experience and skills of a professional silversmith will be available.

For movements without cases it is possible to adapt cases without movements, or make cases from brass, aluminium or perspex. However, this form of collecting is not of universal appeal and if a case is to be made silver is the most attractive material.

Glasses

Watch glasses, as opposed to plastics, should always be fitted to pocket watches. Many watchmakers still carry stocks of glasses and will fit them when purchased. The older type of glass fitted to watches before 1800 which had a flat in the centre (bull's-eye glass) is less common and should be purchased and held as stock against future needs. Watches which should have these glasses are often found with a more modern glass fitted: these glasses will still have a very high dome and should not be lightly discarded but should be replaced with the correct glass and stored for later use.

Dials

Dial repairs are rarely completely satisfactory. All fillers seem to have a different colour or texture to the original dial. An alternative and interesting approach to a watch with a badly damaged dial or without a dial is to make a new one. Again the local school of art and craft will be able to help at the jewellery class where enamelling is practised. It is, however, possible to enamel successfully away from the class because the materials are cheap and the temperatures involved are within the range of the small butane blowlamp.

The new dial should be made from copper sheet about 25 gauge for domed dials and 20 gauge for flat dials (which tend to flex and crack the enamel if made of thinner metal). Mark out the dial, cut to size and drill for hands. Annealing is achieved by heating to red heat and then plunging into cold water. Use a small bolt to hold the dial in the chuck of a power drill and press the dial to a dome shape as the drill rotates. Use a piece of wood to bring pressure to bear on the dial and annealing may be required part way through the doming process. Smooth and clean the domed blank to a good finish and then place in dilute sulphuric acid for a quarter of an hour. After this only handle it with tweezers to avoid grease contamination. Wash the acid-treated blank with water. The acid process can be omitted provided that the blank is completely scale and grease free.

Coat the blank with gum tragacanth (mixed from powder to paste with methylated spirits and diluted with water: ½oz gum to 1qt water), place it on a coarse metal mesh and sieve the white enamel powder through a 60 gauge mesh on to the face. Treat both sides to avoid edges but the butane method burns enamel off the back. Apply the butane lamp to the back of the dial until the enamel fuses at about 820°C. Repeat this process until a satisfactory white finish is obtained. Then draw or paint the numbers with black painting enamel mixed with water to a suitable consistency. Considerable trial and error will be needed until satisfactory draughtsmanship is achieved. The black enamel can be washed off and a new start made as often as required. When satisfied with the lettering the painting enamel must be fired. Painting enamel fuses at a lower temperature than the white enamel (about 730° C) so that there is no problem with the white base. The dial is again heated from the back for at no time should the lamp be played directly on to the face. Sometimes the enamel ground will crack at this late stage in the treatment but in some cases it is possible to salvage the work by fusing new layers of white on top of the numbers and then to paint new ones on.

New feet can be fitted to the back of the dial using Araldite to bond them on or, if preferred, they can be brazed on before enamelling. Enamel repairs to dials with chips are not satisfactory for the enamel does not have the same whiteness as the original and the butane treatment tends to damage the remaining good enamel of the original. The original dial should be put to one side and preserved as part of the watch and a complete replacement made.

Another approach to dial repair which has not been personally tested but which may have possibilities is to use dentist's materials. Colour matching to teeth is reputed to be possible, so that matching to a dial should also be feasible.

GLOSSARY

Arbor   A shaft or axle

Arcaded dial   A dial on which the minute ring has arches between the numerals rather than a circular form

Automatic   Self-winding

Auxiliary compensation   Additional compensation added to a bimetallic balance to reduce middle-temperature error

Back plate   The plate of the watch furthest from the dial

Balance   The oscillating spoked wheel which controls the rate at which the mainspring is allowed to unwind

Balance spring   The spiral or helical spring controlling the balance vibration

Balance staff   The axle on which the balance is fitted

Banking   A system to control the arc of vibration of a balance or, in the lever watch, the motion of the lever

Barrel   The cylindrical container for the mainspring

Beat   The audible tick of the watch. A watch that is in beat has an even tick

Beetle hand   The hour hand used on eighteenth-century watches in combination with the poker minute hand

Bezel   The ring-shaped piece of case holding the glass

Bimetallic balance   A balance wheel whose rim is made of two metals such that the differential expansion rate counteracts the effects of temperature changes on the rate of the watch

Bottom plate   The plate of the watch nearest to the dial

Bow   The hanging ring of a pocket watch

Bull's-eye glass   A high-domed watch glass with a flat centre piece

Button   The winding knob of a keyless watch

Calibre   A term used to denote the size (and shape) of a watch

Cam   A contoured shape which rotates to give a special motion to a follower resting on the cam

Cannon pinion   The pinion driving the motion work with a long hollow arbor which fits over the extended centre-wheel shaft between the dial and the plate

Centre wheel   The second wheel of the train rotating once per hour

Chaffcutter   A Debaufre-type escapement described in Chapter 2

Chapter ring   The ring marked on the dial with hour divisions

Chinese duplex   A duplex escapement watch with double-locking teeth so that two complete balance vibrations are required for escape. The watch advances in increments of one second

Chronograph   A watch with a seconds hand capable of being started, stopped and reset independently of the mean-time hands

Click   A pawl or detent inhibiting motion in one direction

Club-foot verge   A Debaufre-type escapement

Club-tooth lever   A lever escapement with the type of escape wheel described under the Swiss lever in Chapter 2

Cock   A bracket supporting the pivot of a wheel. Usually the term refers to the balance cock for the top balance pivot

Compensated balance   A bimetallic balance designed to counteract the effect of temperature change on the rate of a watch

Contrate wheel   A wheel with teeth at right angles to the plane of the wheel. The fourth wheel in a verge watch is an example

Coqueret   A hard steel bearing on the balance cock of continental watches

Crank lever escapement A Massey lever escapement described in Chapter 2

Crank roller escapement Another name for the crank lever escapement

Crown wheel escapement The verge escapement described in Chapter 2

Curb pins The pins attached to the regulator which loosely hold the balance spring so that its working length can be varied as the regulator is adjusted

Cylinder escapement The first successful alternative to the verge escapement introduced in 1726. It is described in Chapter 2

Dart The safety pointer below the lever fork in the double roller lever watch

Dead beat escapement An escapement without recoil

Dead beat verge A Debaufre-type escapement

Debaufre-type escapement An escapement based on an invention by Peter Debaufre in 1704; it is described in Chapter 2

Deck watch An accurate watch used aboard ship during astronomical observations; it is usually contained in a wooden box

Depth A term to describe the amount of penetration between two meshing gears

Detached escapement An escapement in which the balance vibration is free from friction except during the unlocking and impulse action

Detent A holding piece which stops movement in one or two directions

Detent escapement The (pocket) chronometer escapement described in Chapter 2

Divided lift An escapement in which the lift giving impulse is partly a result of pallet slope and partly as a result of the escape-wheel tooth shape

Double bottom case   A case in which the back opens to reveal a second bottom pierced by a winding hole

Double roller   A lever escapement with two rollers. One roller is for impulse action and the second (smaller) for safety action

Draw   The shaping of the escape wheel teeth so that the lever pallets are drawn into the escape wheel and on to the banking pins to prevent friction due to accidental lever motion

Drop   The free travel of the escape wheel between escape and locking

Duplex escapement   An escapement based on a design by Dutertre described in Chapter 2

Dust cap   A cover placed on the movement in keywind watches

Dutch forgery   A term used to describe watches with a bridge-type balance cock, an arcaded dial with or without a scene and often with a repoussé case. The work is of mediocre quality and marked with an English 'maker'. Probably made partly in England and partly on the Continent

Ébauche   An unfinished movement supplied by a factory to the watchmaker who finishes and signs it

End shake   The axial clearance between a shaft and its bearings

Endstone   A disc-shaped jewel on which the end of the balance top pivot rests

Engine turning   The common form of nineteenth-century case decoration

English lever escapement   The escapement used almost exclusively by English watchmakers from 1850 till 1920; described in Chapter 2

Entry pallet   The pallet on a lever which receives impulse as the escape-wheel teeth enter

Equation of time   The relationship between solar time (based on the position of the sun) and mean time (based on averaged solar motion)

Escapement   The part of a watch movement which constrains the train motion to small increments. It consists of the escape wheel, (lever) and balance

Escape wheel The wheel in the movement connecting with the lever or balance

Exit pallet The pallet on a lever which receives impulse as the escape-wheel teeth leave

Figure plate The small dial indicating the amount of regulation fitted to watches with Tompion regulation

First wheel The great wheel on the fusee or going barrel

Fourth wheel The fourth wheel of the train which rotates once per minute if a seconds hand is fitted

Free sprung A watch with no regulator and curb pins. Regulation is achieved by the timing screws on the balance

Frictional rest escapement An escapement in which the balance motion is affected by friction during the major part of the vibration

Front plate The plate of the watch nearest to the dial

Full plate A watch in which the top plate is complete or has a barrel plate. The balance is fitted on top of the plate

Fusee The conical-shaped piece with a spiral groove for the fusee chain which equalises the mainspring torque

Going barrel A spring barrel driving the watch train without the use of an intermediate fusee and chain

Great wheel The first wheel of the train on the fusee or going barrel

Greenwich time The local mean time at Greenwich used as a basis for longitude and world time-zones

Guard pin The vertical pin (behind the fork on the lever of an English lever escapement) which gives safety action on the roller

Hairspring The balance spring

Half plate A watch in which balance, lever, escape wheel and fourth wheel have separate cocks

Hallmark The assay mark on English silver indicating date and quality

Heart piece   The cam used in a chronograph to reset the centre seconds hand

Hog-bristle regulator   Flexible bristles arranged to limit the arc of vibration of a pre-balance spring watch

Horizontal escapement   The cylinder escapement described in Chapter 2

Horns   The forked end of a lever

Hunter   A watch case with a hinged solid cover over the glass. If fitted with a small glass it is called a half hunter

Impulse   The push given to the balance by the escapement

Index   The regulator pointer

Isochronism   The property of taking the same time for a balance vibration independent of the arc of vibration

Jewels   Bearings made of precious stones such as ruby. Modern jewels are synthetic

Karrusel   A rotating escapement designed to avoid positional error. Described in Chapter 2

Kew Certificate   A rating certificate (A, B and C grade) given by Kew Observatory from 1884

Keyless   A watch that is both wound and hand set without a key

Lancashire size   An English scale for the size of a movement

Lever escapement   A detached escapement described in Chapter 2

Lift   The angular motion of the lever

Ligne   A continental unit of measurement of watch size

Mainspring   The spiral spring in the barrel providing power

Maintaining power   An arrangement in the fusee to keep power on the train whilst the watch is being wound. This avoids the watch stopping or faltering during the operation

Massey lever escapement   A detached lever escapement described in Chapter 2

Mean time   The conventional time shown by clocks and watches based on average solar motion

Middle-temperature error   A residual timekeeping error in watches with a compensated balance

Motion work   The gearing under the dial used to make the hour hand rotate at one twelfth of the speed of the minute hand

Movement   The watch works without case, dial and hands

Oil sink   The small depression in the watch plate around a pivot hole designed to hold oil in place

Ormskirk escapement   A Debaufre-type escapement described in Chapter 2

Overcoil   The last coil of a balance spring which departs from the spiral by being bent above the spring to give a better approach to isochronism. Invented by Breguet

Pair case   A watch with an inner case and a separate outer case. It was in general use until about 1800; uncommon after 1830

Pallet   The part of the escapement through which impulse is transferred from the escape wheel to the balance wheel or lever

Passing crescent   The indentation in the roller in a lever watch to allow the guard pin or dart to pass at the instant of impulse

Pendant   The part of the watch case to which the hanging bow is attached

Pillars   The distance pieces separating the watch plates

Pillar plate   The plate of the watch nearest to the dial

Pinion   A small steel gear wheel (6-12 teeth) driven by a larger brass wheel

Pin lever escapement   An inexpensive lever escapement described in Chapter 2

Pivot   The small diameter part at the end of a shaft which is supported in a bearing

Plates   The flat brass discs supporting the train of the watch. The plates are separated by pillars

Poker hand   The minute hand used on eighteenth-century watches in combination with the beetle hour hand

Positional error   An error due to the variation in the rate of a watch in different positions; pendant up or down, etc

Potence   A hanging bearing such as the lower balance pivot on a full-plate watch

Rack lever escapement   An early lever escapement described in Chapter 2

Ratchet wheel   A wheel with saw-shaped teeth which will rotate in one direction. Rotation in the other direction is impeded by a pawl

Rate   The daily rate of loss or gain of a watch

Recoil   The backward motion of a watch when the escapement is unlocked

Regulation   The term used to describe the adjustment of the timekeeping of a watch

Repeater   A watch which gives audible indication of the approximate time by sounding gongs when a push piece is operated

Rocking bar   A device used to change from winding to hand-setting mode (or vice versa) in keyless watches

Roller   The disc fitted on the balance staff in a lever watch to receive impulse and give safety action

Roskopf escapement   An early pin lever escapement

Safety roller   The smaller roller for safety action in a double-roller lever watch

Savage two-pin escapement   An early lever escapement described in Chapter 2

Second wheel   The centre wheel of the train

Self-winding   A watch with an eccentric weight pivoted so that it will always swing to the low position. The swinging motion winds the watch

Set hands square   The square on the end of the cannon pinion used to set the hands on a keywind watch

Set up   The initial adjustment of tension in a spring

Shifting sleeve   A device used to change from winding to hand-setting mode (or vice versa) in keyless watches

Single roller   A lever watch with a single roller fulfilling both impulse and safety requirements

Solar time   The time indicated by solar position. A day is the time elapsed between two transits of the sun. This is not a constant

Spade hand   An hour hand with an enlarged end of similar shape to the spade symbol on a playing card

Split seconds   A chronograph with two independent seconds hands each of which can be operated separately

Stackfreed   An early regulation device based on the friction between a cam and a spring-loaded follower

Stem wind   Keyless winding and hand setting through a button

Swiss lever escapement   The continental form of lever escapement described in Chapter 2

Table roller lever escapement   The English lever escapement described in Chapter 2

Temperature compensation   Compensation for the changes in timekeeping caused by changes in temperature, usually by bimetallic balance

Terminal curve   The special end shape given to a balance spring to give isochronous motion

Third wheel   The third wheel of the train

Three-quarter plate   A watch in which the balance, lever and escape wheel have separate cocks

Timing screws   The two (or four) screws at the ends of the balance arms (if four, also at right angles to the ends of the arms). They are not compensation screws

Top plate   The plate of the watch furthest from the dial

Tourbillon   A rotating escapement designed to avoid positional error. Described in Chapter 2

Train   The series of meshing wheels and pinions connecting the fusee or going barrel to the escapement

Up-and-down dial   An extra indicator on a watch dial to show the state of mainspring winding

Verge   The vertical staff below the balance wheel carrying the pallets of the verge escapement

Verge escapement   Early escapement described in Chapter 2

Watch paper   A circular piece of paper or cloth often carrying printed information or advertising placed between pair cases by the seller or repairer. The paper takes up play and inhibits rubbing

Wheel   A large, brass, train wheel which drives a smaller steel pinion

Winding square   The square end on the fusee or barrel arbor used for winding a keywind watch

Worm   An 'endless' screw which is rotated to turn a gear placed tangentially to the worm surface. The plane of the gear is that of the worm axis

APPENDIX:
USEFUL INFORMATION

HALLMARKS ON SILVER CASES AS A DATING GUIDE

After about 1700 (Plate Duty Act, 1719), silver cases of English origin, and those of European origin that have passed through an English assay office, will carry a hallmark indicating the metal and the place and year of assay. This system of marks may be used as a guide (reliable or otherwise) to the date of a watch. Watches can be recased and marks can be faked so the information must be treated with care and used in combination with that obtained from other sources such as *Watchmakers and Clockmakers of the World,* G. H. Baillie, 1963. Casemakers' marks, usually consisting of initials, also appear on some cases which may help in dating. European marks are not so easily interpreted but may be used as a guide to the metal quality. The number 800 or 925 indicates the parts per thousand of silver in the case alloy.

On English hallmarked silver the indication of sterling silver (92.5 per cent pure) is a lion passant. There were a number of assay offices but in the period of interest of this book the majority of cases were assayed in London, Birmingham or Chester. These centres are represented by a leopard's head, an anchor and the Chester arms respectively (see the drawing over). Alphabetical letters used in sequence represent the date but they were not changed on the first of January but sometime in mid-year so that dating is not precise. The date-letter style in the sequence A to Z (with some letters occasionally missed out) lasts from twenty to twenty-six years and then the style is changed so that with the aid of an

145

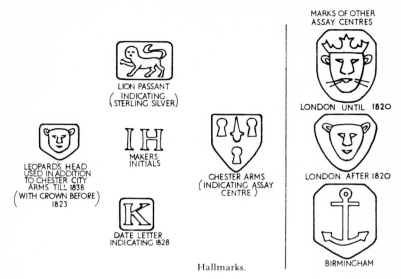

MARKS OF OTHER
ASSAY CENTRES

LION PASSANT
(INDICATING)
(STERLING SILVER)

LONDON UNTIL 1820

LEOPARD'S HEAD
USED IN ADDITION
TO CHESTER CITY
ARMS TILL 1838
(WITH CROWN BEFORE)
1823

I H
MAKERS
INITIALS

CHESTER ARMS
(INDICATING ASSAY
CENTRE)

LONDON AFTER 1820

DATE LETTER
INDICATING 1828

Hallmarks.

BIRMINGHAM

inexpensive book of silver marks or a good memory dating should present no difficulty. Marks are often worn and not very clear but they should appear on each part of the case to obviate this difficulty (on pair cases difference in marks indicates a new or married case). The drawing above shows the marks inside the case of the watch shown on page 96. The method of interpretation of marks is given on the figure.

WEIGHTS AND MEASURES

Jewellers and silversmiths measure in troy weight in which: —
  24 grains make 1 pennyweight (dwt)
  20 pennyweight make 1 ounce troy (oz troy)
  12 ounces troy make 1 pound troy

Thus 1 ounce troy is 480 grains and 1 pound troy is 5760 grains. In the normal avoirdupois system, 1 pound is 16 ounces and 1 pound avoirdupois is 7,000 grains so that 1 ounce avoirdupois is 437½ grains.

In metric measurements 1 pound is 453.6 grams and 1 inch is 25.4 millimetres.

WATCH SIZES

Watch movements of English makers from the second quarter of the nineteenth century onwards carry a size indication stamped on the underside of the dial plate. This consists of a single number between 0 and 40 possibly followed by two numbers written over each other, eg $12\,^0_2$. The first number is the Lancashire watch size which gives the overall movement diameter. To interpret this number, size 0 represents 1 inch and the diameter is 1 inch plus the number of thirtieths of an inch given by the number plus $\frac{5}{30}$ in of 'fall' (the allowance for the larger size of dial plate to allow the top plate to hinge into the case). Thus in the example above the dial plate diameter is $(1 + \frac{12}{30} + \frac{5}{30}) = 1.567$in. The numbers written over each other give the pillar height. To interpret this, size $^0_0$ is 0.125in and if the top number is altered then the height is 0.125in *plus* the number of one hundred and forty-fourths of an inch indicated by the top number. If the bottom number is altered the height is 0.125in *less* the number of one hundred and forty-fourths of an inch indicated by the bottom number. Thus in the example above, the pillar height is $(0.125 - \frac{2}{144}) = 0.111$in. The range of pillar heights is from $^0_6$ to $^{30}_0$ that is from 0.0833in to 0.333in.

Consideration of the history of these sizes would indicate that the sizes were for use with *gauges* rather than in the awkward decimals produced above and that the gauges were based on fractional figures obtained on a system based on twelfths. (See also *Antiquarian Horology*, 2, vol 8, March 1973, 203-4.)

Continental watch sizes are based on *lignes*. A system of units in which 1 ligne is 2.255 millimetres.

WATCHMAKERS

The list below is of surnames of important post-1750 watchmakers. It is not exhaustive. These are names of which a collector should be aware and if he finds a watch with such a

name it would be worth investigating. Much more detail about
the maker must be found. The starting place for this is
Watchmakers and Clockmakers of the World, G. H. Baillie,
1963. It must be appreciated that there are often several
makers with the same surname and it is essential that the
collector is certain about the watch if he is paying for the
name. However, if the watch is offered at the market price for
an anonymous of non-significant maker's piece then purchase
can be made in the hope that research will show a good buy.
The list is restricted to the post-1750 period since it is
considered that *any* watch earlier than this is worth
investigation. No details beyond surname are given so that the
collector is not confused. The recognition of the name is the
first important step.

Arnold	Gout	Mudge
Barraud	Grant	Pendleton
Beatson	Harwood (wrist)	Pennington
Berthoud	Jurgensen	Perrelet
Bonniksen (Karrusel)	Kendall	Philippe
Breguet	Kullberg	Pouzait
Brockbank	Lecoultre	Recordon
Cole	Lepine	Reid
Dent	Leroux	Robin
Dutton	Le Roy	Roscopf (pin lever)
Earnshaw	Leschot	Roskell
Ellicott	Litherland	Savage
Emery	McCabe	Tavan
Frodsham	Margetts	Ulrich
Girard	Massey	Vulliamy

PLACES TO SEE WATCHES

Large collections are usually kept in museums. Many towns
and cities will have such collections and those that are listed
below have been inspected recently. It is not suggested that
these are the only collections available. Smaller collections are

often contained in local museums and galleries. A letter to the local authority before visiting a strange district would probably be beneficial in finding out if such a collection existed. The Antiquarian Horological Society might be a useful source of information for collections abroad. Membership of the society is inexpensive and worthwhile for the quarterly journal. The address of the secretary is given in the bibliography. The society itself does not maintain a collection.

Collections

Basingstoke
Willis Museum and Art Gallery, New Street, Basingstoke
Bury St Edmunds
John Gersham Parkington Memorial Collection, Angel Corner, Bury St Edmunds, Suffolk
Cardiff
Welsh Folk Museum, St Fagans, Cardiff (not at present displayed)
Edinburgh
Royal Scottish Museum, Chambers Street, Edinburgh
Exeter
Royal Albert Memorial Museum, Queen Street, Exeter
London
British Museum, Great Russell Street, London WC1. (A small part of the C. I. Ilbert collection is displayed, the remainder may be available by appointment)
Guildhall Library, Aldermanbury, London, EC2. (The Worshipful Company of Clockmakers collection)
Museum of London, open in 1976, will show watches in their chronological situation rather than as a collection and will incorporate those watches from the old London Museum in Kensington Gardens. The museum is at the corner of London Wall and Aldersgate Street, just north of St Paul's
National Maritime Museum, Romney Road, Greenwich, London, SE10. (Early chronometers)

Science Museum, Exhibition Road, London, SW7
Victoria and Albert Museum, Cromwell Road, London, SW7
Liverpool
Merseyside County Museums, William Brown Street, Liverpool. (A collection of watches and tools)

Markets

Watches can also be seen (and purchased) in markets. Those listed below have been visited and seen to offer numerous watches.

Local markets (usually weekly):
Bath, Cardiff, Stroud, Salisbury, Plymouth, Morecambe, Tavistock

London markets:
Bermondsey market (Caledonian market), Tower Bridge Road, SE1. Opens 0600 on Fridays; Tube station, London Bridge
Petticoat Lane, Middlesex Street, E1. Opens on Sunday morning; Tube station, Aldgate
Portobello Road Market, Portobello Road, W10. Opens on Saturday morning; Tube station, Notting Hill Gate.

Some indoor markets in London:
124 New Bond Street, W1
245-53 King's Road, Chelsea, SW3
26-40 Kensington High Street, W8
49-53 Kensington High Street, W8

PLACES TO BUY WATCH MATERIALS

Parts, tools, fluids, etc:
Local watch repair shops and tool shops, chemists shops
Southern Watch and Clock Supplies Ltd, 48-56 High Street, Orpington, Kent
A. G. Thomas (Bradford) Ltd, 50-2 Heaton Road, Bradford 8, Yorkshire

Enamels:
W. G. Ball Ltd, Anchor Road, Longton, Stoke-on-Trent
Silver, etc:
Johnson, Matthey Metals Ltd, 73 Hatton Garden, London, EC1
Sheffield Smelting Co Ltd, 134 St John Street, London, EC1

SPECIALIST REPAIRERS
Van de Geer Ltd, The Old Rectory, Odstock, Salisbury, Wiltshire

PATENT COPIES
Photocopies of *British Patent Specifications* may be obtained from: Patent Office Sale Branch, Orpington, Kent, BR5 3RD

BIBLIOGRAPHY

Chapter 1
Camerer Cuss, T. P., *The Country Life Book of Watches,* 1967
Camerer Cuss, T. P., *Early Watches,* 1971
Gould, R. T., *The Marine Chronometer,* 1960
Gould, R. T., *John Harrison and His Timekeepers,* 1958
Hayward, J. F., *English Watches,* 1969
Jaquet, E. and Chapuis, A., *The Technique and History of the Swiss Watch,* 1970
Palmer, B., *The Book of American Clocks,* New York, 1950
Quill, H., *John Harrison, the Man who Found Longitude,* 1956
Rees, A., *Clocks, Watches and Chronometers,* Newton Abbot, 1970
Ward, F. A. B., *Time Measurement,* 1970

Chapter 2
Chamberlain, P. M., *It's about Time,* New York, 1941
Clutton, C., and Daniels, G., *Watches,* 1965
Gazeley, W. J., *Clock and Watch Escapements,* 1956

Chapter 3
Baillie, G. H., *Watchmakers and Clockmakers of the World,* 1963
Clutton, C. *et al, Britten's Old Clocks and Watches and Their Makers,* 1973
Cumhaill, P. W., *Investing in Clocks and Watches,* 1967

Chapter 4
de Carle, D., *Clock and Watch Repairing,* 1969
Gazeley, W. J., *Watch and Clock Making and Repairing,* 1965
Rothenberg, P., *Metal Enamelling,* 1969

Appendix
Bradbury, F., *British and Irish Silver Assay Office Marks,* Sheffield, 1950   (pocket book of marks)
Chaffers, W., *Gilda Aurifaborum — A History of English Goldsmiths and Plate Workers and their Marks Stamped on Plate,* 1899
Jackson, C. J., *English Goldsmiths and Their Marks,* New York, 1964
Player, J. W. (Reviser), *Britten's Watch and Clock Makers' Handbook, Dictionary and Guide,* 1955
Stevens, J. C. and Aked, C. K., *Horology in Provincial and Rural Museums,* 1974
Street, E., (editor), *Antiquarian Horology,* quarterly journal of the Antiquarian Horological Society, New House, High Street, Ticehurst, Wadhurst, Sussex, TN5 7AL

ACKNOWLEDGEMENTS

Many people have assisted in the production of this book. Acknowledgements are due to museums for time and correspondence and to acquaintances, friends, collectors and dealers who have helped by loaning watches, chatting, corresponding and advising. Finally the contribution of William R. Milligan who produced all the photographs is gratefully acknowledged.

INDEX